TREASURY OF BIRD LORE

TREASURY
OF
BIRD
LORE

by
Josephine Addison
and illustrated by
Cherry Hillhouse

ANDRE
DEUTSCH

For my sisters
Pauline and Sheila
also Jean

First published in 1998 by
André Deutsch Limited
76 Dean Street
London W1V 5HA
www.vci.co.uk

André Deutsch is a subsidiary of VCI plc

A Catalogue record for this book is available from the British Library

ISBN 0 233 99435 1

Printed in Great Britain by Jarrold Book Printing, Thetford
Reprographics by Jade Reprographics Ltd, Braintree

Contents

BLACKBIRD

When snowdrops die, and the green primrose leaves
Announce the coming flower, the merle's note,
Mellifluous, rich deeped-toned, fills all the vale,
And charms the ravished ear. The hawthorn bush,
New-budded, is his perch; there the grey dawn
He hails; and there, with parting light, concludes
His melody.
'The Birds of Scotland' JAMES GRAHAME (1763-1811)

BLACKBIRD *(Turdus Merula)*. This gregarious member of the thrush family can be found in many parts of Britain throughout the year. The resident population are joined in the autumn by large numbers of migrants en route to warmer climates. They descend on the east coast regions from Northern Europe, often staying on to enjoy the remnants of the apple orchards, abundance of berries and generous bird-tables. The poet Joseph Addison wrote of the birds.

I value my garden for being full of blackbirds than of cherries,
and very frankly give them fruit for their song.

It appears that the name blackbird was first mentioned in 1486. According to the *Oxford Dictionary of Bird Names* it cannot be older than 1300, since it reflects that stage in the evolution of the meaning of the word bird, when it applied to small birds, but not yet to larger ones – crows and ravens were referred to as black fowls – replacing the traditional ouzel. Black ouzel was a name common in Lancashire, Yorkshire and Worcestershire, and blackie was in general use as a pet form of blackbird. Other names included merle, ouzel and woosel.

Nesting in woodlands, hedgerows and gardens it has, as John Clare, the nature poet recalled, 'a thousand whims in choosing places for her nest' which is made of mud and moss, lined with grasses in which three to five bluish-green, brown-speckled eggs are laid. In his poem 'Summer Shower' Clare noted a

> *... blackbird squatting in her mortared nest*
> *Safe hid in ivy and the pathless wood*
> *Pruneth her sooty breast*
> *And warms her downy brood.*

Although this is a modest description of the female bird, it is a marked contrast to the entirely jet-black plumage of the male bird, with his crocus-coloured bill and smart matching eye ring. Blackbirds are a familiar sight in the garden when – with head cocked as though listening but actually watching, almost daring an unsuspecting worm to leave the safety of the earth – an unfairly matched tug-of-war follows.

Earlier this century, however, the hunter became the hunted. In an effort to decrease the number of blackbirds before the start of the breeding season, boys would walk either side of a hedge, which tended to deter the birds from flying out, by which time they were in range of the catapults. Another means of capture was to scatter corn near the barn doors and then drop a net from the upper granary door. In earlier times catching blackbirds had another purpose as they also provided food for the family, as well as entertainment. According to the old nursery rhyme:

> *Sing a song of sixpence*
> *A pocket full of rye*
> *Four and twenty*
> *blackbirds*
> *Baked in a pie.*

This verse literally means what it says, referring to the medieval custom of hiding birds in a pie. During the preparation, part of the pie was cooked 'blind' and the live birds were added just prior to serving, providing amusing entertainment and possibly consternation to the assembled guests as they took flight. A recipe for cooking blackbird consisted of the following instructions; 'Take small birds, and pluck, and draw them clean, and wash them well, and chop off the legs and fry them in a pan of fresh grease right well. Then lay them on a fair cloth, and let the grease run out. Then take onions, and mince them small, and fry them in fair fresh grease, and cast them in an earthen pot. Then take a good portion of cinnamon and wine, and dry through a strainer, and cast into the pot with the onions. Then cast the birds thereto, and the cloves and the mace, and a little quantity of powdered pepper thereto, and let them boil together enough. Then cast thereto sugar, powdered ginger, salt, saffron and serve forth.' Blackbird flesh is said to be aromatic in flavour and slightly bitter.

The blackbird who habitually hops is not only a good mimic but also the only bird that whistles, as Michael Drayton remarked: 'Upon his dulcet pype the Merle doth onely play.' Weather-lorists noted the quality of the sound of this excellent songster. 'When the voices of blackbirds are unusually shrill, or when the blackbirds sing much in the morning rain will follow'. According to E Darwin (although it is also attributed to Dr Jenner):

Though June, the air is cold and still,
The merry blackbird's voice is shrill;
And from Meath:
When the blackbird sings before Christmas,
She will cry before Candlemas.

There are those who have mixed feelings about the song of the blackbird as a recent poem, 'Twang', by Rita Holroyd suggests:

When blackbirds pierce the calm of dawn
and wake me with their call
I long for arrows and a bow

> *to silence one and all.*
> *But when their song at eventide*
> *has soothed my worried mind*
> *the thought I harboured earlier*
> *seems terribly unkind.*

In folklore blackbird means bad luck, evil and temptation and typifies the devil or underworld deity. Nevertheless if you see the bird on St Valentine's Day it is said you will marry a priest. The blackbird was one of many birds who featured in traditional, oral rhymes and riddles.

> *As I went over the water,*
> *The water went over me.*
> *I saw two little blackbirds*
> *Sitting on a tree,*
> *The one called me a rascal,*
> *The other called me a thief;*
> *I took up my little black stick,*
> *And knocked out all their teeth.*

And

> *There were two blackirds sitting on a hill,*
> *The one named Jack, the other named Jill*
> *Fly away, Jack! Fly away Jill*
> *Come again, Jack! Come again Jill!*

In the Jacobite song, The 'Chief Blackbird', the reference is to Charles II.

> *Once in fair England my blackbird did flourish;*
> *He was the chief blackbird that in it did spring.*
> *Prime ladies of honour his person did nourish*
> *For blackbird was truly the son of a king.*
> *But since that false fortune, which still is uncertain,*
> *Has caused this parting between him and me,*
> *His name I'll advance in Spain and in France*
> *And I'll seek out my blackbird wherever he be.*

BLUE TIT

Where is he, that giddy sprite,
Blue cap, with his colours bright,
Who was blest as bird could be,
Feeding in the apple tree;
Made such wanton spoil and rout,
Turning blossoms inside out;
'The Kitten and Falling Leaves',
WILLIAM WORDSWORTH

BLUE TIT *(Parus caerulus)*. The name blue tit was established in 1843 by the ornithologist and author of *British Birds*, William Yarrell (1871-1875) for the older blue titmouse, which was referred to, in 1678 as 'the blue titmouse, or nun.' The adjective blue also occurs in local names for this bird, such as blue bonnet and blue cap. The term denotes a cap of blue material, but it was also applied to a servant or tradesman, who traditionally wore such a cap. This name went out of fashion by 1700. The word tit is an abbreviation of titmouse, the family name for this species, and came into Middle English from the Icelandic, *titir* – a small bird.

Names for the blue tit which refer to its delightful plumage include blue ox-eye, blue spick and blue yaup, and some of those in general use are tom tit, bee bird, billy biter, pickcheese tidife yaup and pinchem.

The habitat of the blue tit covers broadleaf woods, especially birch and oak, as well as gardens where they build nests of moss, grass and bark strips, lined with downy feathers, in holes, cavities and nest boxes. A nest box on an oak tree would probably be the ideal home. John Clare describes an alternative site:

11

> *The blue cap hid in the lime kilns out of sight*
> *Lays nine small eggs and spotted red and white*
> *And oft in walls where boys a noisey pest*
> *Will pull a stone away to get the nest.*

Although frequently seen pecking off young buds blue tits are very clever feeders, often swinging precariously by their feet under branches looking upwards for hidden treasures, or performing acrobatic manoeuvres on the end of fine twigs.

> *. . . the bluecap tootles in its glee*
> *Picking the flies from orchard apple tree.*

Perhaps their least endearing trick, due to an unusual partiality to cream, is when they peck holes in milk bottle tops! They are colourful and smart in their bright blue plumage – the nape, wings and tail are a darker shade – topped by an azure cap with a white halo and distinctive yellow breast. The blue tit is a welcome sight on any bird table or swinging casually from a coconut shell.

> *Lithest, gaudiest Harlequin!*
> *Prettiest tumbler ever seen!*

According to weather lore the 'titmouse foretells cold, if crying "Pincher".' The great tit (Parus major), although found in a similiar habitat, is easily distinguished from the smaller blue tit, having a glossy black cap, collar and a scarf, which divides its yellow breast plumage.

> *Under the twigs the black cap hangs in vain*
> *The snow white patch streaked over either eye*
> *This way and that he turns and peeps again*
> *As wont where silk-cased insects used to lie*
> *The black cap builds in trees where boys can see,*
> *The eggs and scarce get finger in the tree.*

wrote John Clare in his poem 'The Blackcap'.

Other enemies are on the prowl too – magpies and sparrowhawks. The great tit is also known as black cap lolly, black-headed Bob, and black-headed Tomtit. And from its rasping song, which has all the exciting sounds of an ancient bicycle pump in action, saw sharpener, sit ye down and pridden pal.

Many different calls have been described for this species and it is said that if you do not recognize a particular sound in a wood it will be a great tit. It is also known as big ox-eye, Joe Ben and Tom noup. Great tits are the bully boys of the tit family and can be quite aggresive, especially when feeding. (The species do feed together.) One threat posture is 'horizontal' with the wings and the tail fanned – sometimes the bill is open; another is 'vertical' with the wing feathers drooping down and the chin held high. In autumn and winter great tits roam the woods in flocks, dropping to the ground for occasional leaf turning and poking around of moss and fungi in their search for food.

The blue tits' search for food is not always to be found in such pleasant surroundings. In 1789 Gilbert White wrote to fellow naturalist Thomas Pennant of the bird: 'Beside insects, it is very fond of flesh; for it frequently picks on dunghills: it is a vast admirer of suet, and haunts butcher's shops. When a boy, I have known twenty on a morning caught with snap mouse-traps, baited with sallow or suet.' A far cry from the memories of Walter de la Mare in 'Tomtit':

> *When tapping at the window-pane,*
> *My visitor has come again*
> *To peck late supper at his ease –*
> *A morsel of suspended cheese.*

BUZZARD

BUZZARD *(Buteo buteo)*. The name was first recorded in 1300 as 'busard', the present spelling dating from 1616 from the French *busard,* and has been known since the twelfth century. Regional names for the bird include bald kite, buzzard hawk, gled, the glider, shreak, puttock, puddock and bascud.

The sailing puddock sweeps about for prey
And keeps above the woods from day to day.

A modern name, tourists' eagle, is said to be an ironic invention by the Scots as visitors apparently constantly mistake the bird for the golden eagle.

The fate of this large bird of prey, which can be seen in the hilly countryside and wooded farmland of western Britain, the Lake District and Scotland, has in the past largely depended on the activity of gamekeepers and the supply of disease-free rabbits. Egg collectors and specimen hunters have also added to its decline. Today it is vulnerable to poisoned baits – more buzzards are killed this way than any other raptor in Britain. Although the buzzard is smaller than a golden eagle it is the commonest large bird of prey in Britain. The birds have eyes the size of a human's. The female is larger than the male but they have similar plumage: soft chestnut-brown upper-parts and mottled brown and white under-parts with unfeathered yellow legs. When soaring, the birds display with great effect their broad, rounded wings with 'finger-tips' spread and barred fanned tail.

> *Then, with a sudden lift of the one great pinion,*
> *Swung proudly to a curve*
> *and from its height*
> *Took half a mile of*
> *sunlight in one long sweep*

continued Martin Armstrong. According to the ornithologist Derwent May, their mating rituals are conducted in the sky with the male circling the female, always looking straight into her face. Sometimes the male will dive wildly past her and then swoop up again, their talons touching in the excitement of the duel. They nest from ground level up to fifty feet in a tree – favouring ones with ivy-covered trunks – or on high crags and rocky ledges overlooking the sea. The nest is a bulky structure of sticks, heather, bracken, moss and bark, which is decorated from time to time by the female with fresh oak twigs bearing green leaves.

> *They make a nest so large in*
> *woods remote*
> *Would fill a woman's apron with the*
> *sprotes*
> *And schoolboys daring doing*
> *tasks the best*

Will often climb and stand upon the nest.
. . . almost big enough to make a bed,

wrote John Clare in his *Journal*. They lay two or three white or bluish-coloured eggs with reddish-brown blotches:

And lay three eggs and spotted o'er with red
The schoolboy often hears the old ones cry
And climbs the tree and gets them ere they fly
And takes them home and often cuts their wing
And ties them in the garden with a string

continued the poet, drawing attention to an almost unbelievably cruel practice. When humans get too close to the nest of a buzzard it will make passing swoops at the intruder then fly off to warn its mate, making loud mewing cries. There is usually only one brood. The naturalist Gilbert White, in his *Natural History and Antiquities of Selborne*, observed 'kites and buzzards sail round in circles with wings expanded and motionless'. Although they are usually seen in flight, where with their large eyes they are able to observe their diet of frogs, rabbits and voles, they do spend most of their time perched. However an old Fen song recalls old habitats:

Pray, sirs, consider had you been
Bred where whole winters nothing's seen
But naked floods for miles and miles,
Except a boat the eye beguiles,
Or coots, in clouds, by Buzzards teaz'd,
Your ear with seeming thunder seized
From rais'd decoy – there ducks on flight
By tens of thousands darken sight.

CHAFFINCH

Oh, to be in England
Now that April's there,
And whoever wakes in England
Sees, some morning, unaware,
That the lowest boughs and the brushwood sheaf
Round the elm-tree bole are in tiny leaf,
While the chaffinch sings on the orchard bough
In England – now!
'Home Thoughts From Abroad', ROBERT BROWNING

CHAFFINCH *(Fringilla coelebs)*. Chaffinch is a traditional name going back to Old English 'ceaffinc'; the bird would often be seen around the threshing floor or at the barn door searching for grain among the chaff. Despite many synonyms such as dapfinch, a Devon name reflecting the local verb dap, hop, move briskly, pie finch, scobby and spink the present word has long been the chief name. A pet form, chaffie may occur locally. Nevertheless there are numerous regional names, some reflecting the sound of the birds, including chink chaffey, pink twink, shiltie and shilfa which the Scottish poet James Grahame (1765-1811) describes seeing in woodland:

When not a strain is heard through all the woods
I've seen the shilfa light from off his perch
And hop into a shallow of the stream,
Then, half afraid, flit to the shore, then in
Again alight and dip his rosy breast,
And fluttering wings, while dew-like globules
The plumage of his brown empurpled back.

From the colour of its plumage come such delightful names as copper finch, apple sheelie, white wing and fleckiewing. Boldie, scobb, wheatsel, brisk finch and wet bird add to the list of names used for this common and widespread species.

The name wet bird reflects its plaintive cry 'weet weet,' considered by many to foretell rain and 'dreep dreep' supposedly the sound of rain.

Weet-weet!
Dreep-dreep!

The rhyme itself is so brief that unless one was familiar with the context it cannot be understood. When children heard the bird they would first imitate it then refer to it in rhyme and no doubt await the outcome!

This popular early spring songster with its familiar anxious 'pink pink' call and rattling song – which ends with a flourish – favours the hedgerows of gardens and farmland.

Chaffinches dropping on the oats
Toss up and down like little boats

wrote Andrew Young in 'Denholme Dene'. Their beautifully constructed nest is fashioned from grass, moss, bark fibres, bits of paper and roots decorated with lichen and cobwebs, and lined with hair. The eggs, four to five in number, are greenish-brown to blue in colour with dark markings. There are vigorous outbursts of song when males occupy their territories and the nest is eventually built near one of their regular song posts. They nest in low bushes and trees, and sometimes against a wall or fence in a creeper or shrub. The male is a very attractive bird with a greyish-blue head and pinkish-brown cheeks, chestnut mantle, green rump and

pinkish-brown breast with a broad white epaulette on his shoulder, narrow white wing bar and white outer tail feathers. Although somewhat overshadowed by her partner, the plumage of the female, soft greenish-brown with paler under-parts, is smartly understated. John Clare recalls the age old problem when unthinking schoolboys find a chaffinch nest. In this instance he uses the rural name pink:

At length they got agen a bush to play
And found a pink's nest round and mossed with grey
And lined about with feathers and with hair
They tryed to climb but brambles said forbear
One found a stone and stronger than the rest
And took another up to reach the nest
Heres eggs they hollowed with a hearty shout
Small round and blotched they reached and tore them out
The old birds sat and hollowed pink pink pink
And cattle hurried to the pond to drink.

An unusual nesting place was reported in the Buckingham-shire Herald in 1792, in 'a block or pulley, near the the head of the mast of a gabbert, now lying near Broomielaw, there is a chaffinch's nest and four eggs. The nest was built while the vessel lay at Greenock, and was followed hither by both birds. Though the block is occasionally lowered for inspection of the curious, the birds have not forsaken the nest.' The story inspired Thomas Cowper to write a long poem, 'A Tale Founded On Fact', also touching on the superstitious nature of seamen;

In Scotland's realm, where trees are few,
Nor even shrubs abound
But where, however bleak the view,
Some better things are found.

For seamen much believe in signs
And from a chance so new
Each some approaching good divines
And may his hopes be true.

CORMORANT

... below on a rock against the grey sea fretted,
Pipe-necked and stationary silhouetted,
Cormorants stood in a wise, black, equal row
Above the nests and long blue eggs we know.
'The Birds', JOHN COLLINGS SQUIRE

CORMORANT (*Phalacrocorax carbo*). The name first appeared in 1320 as cormerant and in 1381 as cormeraunt. The modern spelling, followed by a temporary deviation in 1768, corvorant, was established in 1678. The source of the name is French, the oldest known form being 'cormareg'. Local names include hiblin, which is a Manx name, huplin and lairblade from the Orkneys, lorin and white lorin from the Shetlands, and parson from the south coast of England; (alluding to the sombre clerical plumage and stance with wings outstretched). Percy Bysshe Shelley penned a more dramatic description of this bird of ill-omen in 'The Witch of Atlas':

... the flagging wing
Of the roused cormorant in the lightning flash
Looked like the wreck of some wind-wandering
Fragment of inky thunder-smoke.

This handsome bird with its glossy black, blue and bronze plumage, highlighted in courtship by a flashy white throat and thigh patch, breeds on rocky coasts in Britain and trees in Ireland. They nest in colonies on cliff edges in loosely defined piles of twigs and seaweed, lined with soft vegetation, laying three or four chalky white eggs. The combination of crystal sharp eyesight and the modified barbs on the feathers enable cormorants to see and swim under water, bringing their catch to the surface to shake or toss before swallowing.

The cormorant then comes (by his devouring kind)
Which flying o'er the fen immediately doth find
The fleet best stored of fish, when from his wings at full
As though he shot himself into the thick'ned skull,
He under water goes and so the shoal pursues

wrote Michael Drayton in 'Polyolbion'. The cormorant is said to eat twice its own weight of fish each day, and although much of their diet is of no commercial value they are still persecuted by fishermen. Chaucer refers to the bird as 'The hote cormorant of gluttony' while other references have 'the greedy cormorant'. Nevertheless the bird's fishing ability is well known throughout the world, particularly in China and Japan. Here, tame birds were restrained by a leather collar and lead, which prevented them swallowing fish, as they dived off the fishing boats into the sea. Although this strange method of fishing was and still is practised in some parts of Asia, something similar, but considered a sport, was formerly practised in Europe – a type of underwater falconry. Cormorants which formerly flourished in England were exploited under the patronage of the Stuart kings, especially James I. Fortunately, the Master of the Royal Cormorants no longer has a tenant.

Iron Age fowlers are alleged to have hunted the cormorant without, one assumes, the advice given in the medieval recipe when cooking the bird:

The cormorant shall be roasted I point out
With the bill kept on for a great countess.

In folklore the cormorant symbolizes greed and was regarded as a bird of ill-omen:

. . . and towards the mystic ring
Where Augurs stand, the Future questioning,
*   Slowly the cormorant aims her heavy flight,*
*   Portending ruin to each baleful rite*
That, in the lapse of ages, hath crept o'er
Diluvian truths, and patriarchal lore

21

wrote William Wordsworth in 'Trepidation of the Druids'. A more recent confirmation of such a belief was recorded on 9 September 1860 when 'a cormorant took up its position on the steeple of Boston church (possibly the Stump) in Lincolnshire, much to the alarm of the superstitious. There it remained with the exception of two hours' absence until early on May morning, when it was shot by the caretaker of the church. The fears of the credulous were singularly confirmed when the news arrived of the loss of the Lady Elgin at sea with three hundred passengers, amongst whom were Mr Ingram, member for Boston, and his son, on the very morning when the bird was first seen.' In weather lore strong winds were indicated by the movement of the bird:

> *When crying cormorants forsake the sea,*
> *And, stretching to the covert, wing their way.*

And as a sign of bad weather:

> *And diving cormorants their wings expand*
> *And tread – strange visitors – the solid land.*

An amusing anonymous fantasy poem connects the bird with lightning.

> *The common cormorant or shag*
> *Lays eggs inside a paper bag,*
> *The reason you will see no doubt –*
> *It is to keep the lightning out.*
> *But what these unobservant birds*
> *Have never noticed is that herds*
> *Of wandering bears may come with buns*
> *And steal the bags to hold the crumbs.*

CORNCRAKE

While Landrails call from day to day
Amid the grass and grain
We hear it in the weeding time
When knee deep waves the corn
We hear it in the summer's prime
Through meadows night and morn.
'Landrail', JOHN CLARE

CORNCRAKE *(Crex crex)*. One of the earliest references to the bird seems to be corne crake in 1455, then cornecraik in 1552. Originally Scottish, the name entered English ornithological literature through Thomas Bewick (Bewick's Swan) in 1797 in his *History of British Birds*. Crake is a common local name for the corn crake, imitative of the monotonous rasping croak which has been likened to the teeth of a comb being drawn rapidly across the edge of a matchbox, twice, tolerable from a distance, harsher nearby. Land-rail, which is an alternative name for the corncrake, was first used in 1678 and taken from the Latin *Rallus terrestris,* which in 1786 was replaced by crake gallinule. Gallinule was introduced as a generic term which also included the moorhen, and the spotted corncrake. Nevertheless landrail was still in use during this century.

A possible rescue plan for this unusual rare bird now

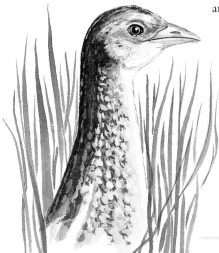

teetering on the verge of extinction, has been mounted in South Yorkshire, England. This year several pairs of corncrake have been released on a nature reserve in a desperate attempt to re-establish the birds. The corncrake has numerous country names, many reflecting its natural habitat, while others refer to its distinctive 'crekking' call.

> *The fairy like and seldom-seen land rail*
> *Utters 'craik craik' like voices underground*
> *Right glad to meet the evening's dewy veil*
> *And see the light fade into glooms around*

wrote John Clare in 'Summer Moods'. Other names include grass quail, grass drake, corn drake, meadow drake and crake, land hen, gorse duck, gallwell drake and hay crake. It is also known as rape-scrape, creck, cracker and craker. The corncrake closely resembles a moorhen in shape but has yellowish-buff upper parts and fainter coloured eye streaks, reddish-brown barring on its flanks and near the tail. Chestnut wings show up in flight, which it undertakes for short distances with legs dangling in rather an ungainly manner. Their nest, a hollow lined with grass in dense tussocks – tent-like – conceals eight to twelve creamy-coloured eggs with brown markings. If one is fortunate enough to see this former woodland bird, it will be in a hay meadow or cornfield where it has safely enjoyed a habitat, ironically cultivated by farmers, over the centuries. Nowadays modern practices, such as the early cutting of hay meadows for silage which destroys nests or prevents young birds escaping, and over-grazing of grassland, have all contributed towards the disappearance of the corncrake. The exception is western Ireland and the northern and western islands of Scotland, where it can be heard in spring after a long-haul flight from Central Africa. The Scottish poet Robert Burns (1759-96) makes reference to the corncrake in his 'Elegy On Captain Matthew Henderson':

Mourn, clamouring crakes at close o'day
'Mang fields o'flowering claver gay;
And when ye wing your annual way
Frae our cauld shore,
Tell thae warlds wha lies in clay,
Wham we deplore.

The slow decline of the corncrake began many years ago. During the early part of the nineteenth century John Clare was writing of the dangers facing the bird:

Yet accidents will often meet
The nest within its way
And weeders when they weed the wheat
Discover where they lay.

Their nests, befitting a secretive bird, are difficult to find. Clare wrote of the excitement, discovering one in later life:

But great the joy I missed in youth
As not to find them then
For when a boy new nest meets
Joy gushes in his breast
Nor would his heart so quickly beat
Were guineas in the nest.

As with all wild birds the corncrake was trapped as a source of food. Like the quail, wheatear and lark it was served whole. An early nineteenth century recipe advised that the bird should first be drawn and wiped clean with a wet cloth, trussed with the head under the wing and the thighs close to the sides, with a small skewer run through the body to keep the legs straight. A dish of five corncrakes required a quarter of a pound of butter, fried breadcrumbs and a little good gravy. To cook the birds 'place before a fire and baste them constantly with butter. They will take about a quarter of an hour or twenty minutes to roast, and when done, place them on a layer of fried bread crumbs, on a very hot dish. Serve with a tureen of bread sauce, and one good gravy.'

CUCKOO

Not the whole warbling grove in concert heard
When sunshine follows shower, the breast can thrill
Like the first summons, Cuckoo! of thy bill,
With its twin notes inseparably paired.
'To the Cuckoo', WILLIAM WORDSWORTH

CUCKOO *(Cuculus canorus)*. The name was brought to this country by the Normans; it is Old French, cucu, replacing the Old English 'geac' and, Middle English 'yek', which survived until the fifteenth century. Although this traditionally English name cuckoo was replaced in the north of England by its Norse cognate *gowk*, it was formerly cuckow. The old name first appears in what is said to be the oldest song in the English language, written by a monk at Reading Abbey in 1240 to show how men's hearts respond to the influences of spring.

Summer is icumen in
Llude sing cuccu
Spryngeth sed and bloweth mede
And groweth the wude nu.

In 1381 Chaucer chose cokkow, although other manuscripts had cucko, kukkowe, cuccow and cuckow. The latter was the most frequently used, surviving until the nineteenth century. However, the seventeenth century spelling 'cuckoe' or 'guckoe', where oe was pronounced shoe, emphasized the imitative character of the name. Common names include geck, hobby, Welsh ambassador, gawky gog and gok.

The cuckoo can be seen in woods, on farm and moorland and in reed beds. Nest building is not a problem for the cuckoo, as they are brood parasites – laying their eggs in the nests of other birds, usually fifteen to twenty, one per nest. The colour of the egg varies, resembling those of the unsuspecting foster parent. The newly hatched cuckoo ejects any young or eggs, becoming the sole occupant of the nest which it will in due course fill.

The male and female bird are similiar in colour, slim blue-grey birds with pointed wings and long tail with brown barred lower breast and belly like a sparrowhawk.

The arrival of the bird in spring, with the familiar male call and bubbling chuckle of the female, is traditionally 14 April in Sussex. Here it is known as Cuckoo Day, when it is advisable to turn over your money so that you will never be in need of it. Prior to this date there is a flurry of correspondence to The Times newspaper which publishes, annually, letters of early sightings which are sometimes confused with the call of the dove.

One old rhyme, of which there are many variations, not only indicates the months associated with the cuckoo's presence but also the change in tone of the bird's song.

In April come he will
In May he sings all day
In June he changes tune
In July he prepares to fly
In August go he must
If he stays till September
Tis as much as the oldest man can ever remember.

A briefer more up to date version reveals:

The cuckoo comes in April
Sings the month of May

> *Changes its tune in the middle of June*
> *And in July he flies away.*

The writer Hayward (1587) was less flattering but to the point:

> *In Aprill, the koscoo can sing her song by rote*
> *In June, of tune she cannot sing a note:*
> *At first koo-coo, koo-coo, sing still can she do;*
> *At last, kooke, kooke; six kookes to one koo*

Where the cuckoo went in August was a puzzle. Many people believed they hibernated in tree stumps, others that they changed into hawks, a likeness noted by John Clare:

> *The cuckoo like a hawk in flight*
> *With narrow pointed wings*
> *Wews oer our heads – soon out of sight.*

In folklore the cuckoo is a symbol of adultery, cuckoldry, egoism, insanity, selfishness and usurpation. The bird is also a harbinger of spring. The sight and sound of the cuckoo is a good omen for marriage, thus it is also seen as a bird of love. Should you wish to know whom you will marry, take off your shoe when you first hear the cuckoo and you will find a hair the same colour as that of your future spouse.

> *Upon a rising bank I sat adown,*
> *Then doffed my shoe, and by my troth, I swear,*
> *Therein I spied this yellow frizzled hair*

wrote John Gay in 'The Shepherd's Week'. If you count the number of 'cuckoos' the first time you hear it, you will know answers to the question: how many years will pass before marry. How many children will I have? And, if these events have passed, how many years before I die! Another superstition stated that whatever state of health you are in when you hear the first cuckoo of the year, you will remain so for the rest of the year. A useful tip for those plagued by fleas was recommended by Pliny. On hearing the first two notes of the cuckoo 'pick up the earth lying within the compass of his right footprint, it will prove a sovran remedy'.

The nesting practice of the cuckoo is associated with the Elizabethan word cuckold, which simply means husband of an adulteress, a man whose wife has proved unfaithful; an allusion to the female cuckoo's habit of laying her eggs in the nest of other birds. Some say the allusion is to the ancient custom of calling 'ku-ku,' to warn a husband that an adulterer was approaching, and that with time the term began to apply to the husband himself. From *Love's Labour's Lost*:

> *The cuckoo then on every tree*
> *Mocks married men, for thus sings he 'Cuckoo'.*

The fate of the foster mother when the cuckoo is grown was that it devoured her or, as the Roman writer Pliny says, 'bit off her head'. Reference is made to this in Chaucer's 'The Parliament of Fowls', referring to it as the hedge sparrow:

> *Thou murderer of the heysoge on the branch*
> *That brought thee forth, thou ruthless glutton.*

However an anonymous eighth century riddle suggests otherwise:

> *My foster mother fed me and then,*
> *When I was strong enough to set out on my own,*
> *I deserted her, so of daughters and sons,*
> *She had fewer in spite of all she had done.*

Much of the surviving lore reflects the amount of advice available to farmers at this important time of year with spring sowing and the outcome of the harvest:

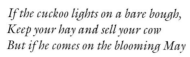

If the cuckoo lights on a bare bough,
Keep your hay and sell your cow
But if he comes on the blooming May

Keep your cow and sell your hay.
If the cuckoo sings when the hedge is brown
Sell thy horse and buy thy corn.

If the cuckoo sings when the hedge is green
Keep thy horse and sell thy corn
If the cuckoo does not cease singing at midsummer,
corn will be dear.

Spring gales about the time of the equinox have been called 'gowk storms', because they follow the cuckoo.

The cuckoo comes in mid March and cucks in mid April:
And goes away at Lammas-tide, when the corn begins to fill.

A more precise forecast can be given when the cuckoo is heard on 21 June – we can expect a wet summer. In Scotland when the cuckoo is heard in the lowlands it indicates rain; on high lands, fair weather.

In plant lore there are several flowers associated with the cuckoo – marsh marigold blows when the cuckoo sings. It was said to have its bread and meat in the shape of the wood sorrel *(Panis cuculi)*. The wild arum is known as cuckoo-pint, the cuckoo flower or lady's smock *(Cardamine pratensis)* also ragged robin *(Lychnis flos-cuculi)*. William Shakespeare refers to another one:

And Lady-smocks all silver white,
And Cuckoo buds of yellow hue
Do paint the meadows with delight.

This may have been a reference to golden-coloured buttercups. Incidentally, cuckoo was prepared and cooked in a similiar manner to larks.

EAGLE

He clasps the crag with crooked hands;
Close to the sun in lonely lands,
Ringed with the azure world, he stands.
The wrinkled sea beneath him crawls;
He watches from his mountain walls,
And like a thunderbolt he falls.
'The Eagle', Alfred, LORD TENNYSON.

GOLDEN EAGLE *(Aquila chrysaetos)*. The common name eagle goes back to Middle English 'egle' and has been known since 1385. The present spelling first appears in 1555 in a reference to 'erens or eagles'. It remained so until the English writer and naturalist, Ray adopted the name Golden Eagle in 1678 and from that time was used by succeeding authors.

During the last century, like many of Britain's rarer raptors, it was seriously persecuted and can now only be found soaring majestically in the mountainous regions of Scotland and possibly the Lake District.

He hangs between his wings outspread
Level and still
And bends a narrow golden
head,
Scanning the ground to
kill.

Yet as he sails and
smoothly swings
Round the hillside,
He looks as though
from his own wings
He hung down crucified

wrote Andrew Young in 'The Eagle'.

The golden eagle is Britain's largest bird of prey, with chestnut-coloured plumage although the flat crown and shaggy hind neck are washed golden brown, accentuating the massive bill. Ankle length feathered trousers reveal deadly taloned toes. They nest on remote crags or occasionally Scots pine, enjoying a magnificent view of the their extensive territory. The nest – of which they have between two and four alternative sites which they use if their eyrie becomes fouled – is a bulky construction of branches, heather, bracken lined with grasses to which fresh greenery is added during the season. They lay, usually two, whitish or blotched brown eggs.

The eagle symbolizes ascension, aspiration, empire, faith, faithfulness, fertility, freedom, fortitude, generosity, immortality, inspiration, keeness of vision, majesty, power, swiftness, storm, victory, splendour and strength. Alternatively it symbolizes evil, discord and rapacity. It typifies deity, fire, storm, wind and lightning; and as king of the birds, the element air, and the sun as it takes its daily flight across the sky. As it is, according to legend, the only bird capable of gazing at the sun without being dazzled, this has been interpreted to mean that it is capable of contemplating divine splendour. In medieval legend an old eagle flies into the fiery regions of the sun; his feathers are burnt off and he falls into a fountain where his youth is renewed; thus the eagle typifies physical and spiritual regeneration. Because of its claws, it is invariably identified in ancient zodiacs with the crab (Cancer) the chaos principle, and with Scorpio, the evil principle. The constellation Aquila in the southern sky is also known as the Eagle.

In Greek mythology an eagle brought nectar to Zeus, chief of the gods, when he was hidden from Cronus. The eagle was also the steed of the youth Ganymede. Zeus, struck by his wondrous beauty, gave his father six fine horses for him and sent his eagle to transport Ganymede to Olympus, where he was made one of the immortals and replaced Hebe as cup-bearer to the gods.

In Roman mythology it is an aspect of Jove. As birds were widely believed to be the spirits of the dead, the Romans used

to set free an eagle over a funeral pyre so that the spirit of the deceased could enter the bird and be conducted to heaven.

The ancient Hebrews, who noted the careful pains the bird took in teaching its young to fly, believed that it exemplified God's providential care over Israel.

Before the feathers of her younglings grow,
She lifts them one by one from out their nest
To view the sun, thereby her own to know.
Those that behold it not with open eye,
She lets them fall, not able yet to fly,

wrote Thomas Watson (1557-1592) in 'My Love Is Past'. In the Christian tradition the eagle typifies salvation and was assigned to the apostle St John; the lion to St Mark, the calf to St Luke and the beast with a man's head to St Matthew. The church lectern from which the gospel is read is often designed in the form of this impressive bird. The eagle also symbolizes the Lord and Leader of Hosts, the Sevenfold Spirit. A fluttering eagle in Christianity represents the promise 'They that wait upon the Lord shall mount up with wings as eagles'. A two-headed eagle symbolizes creative power and omniscience and in the Christian tradition the holy spirit of God. The two-headed eagle was the emblem of the joining of the Holy Roman Empire; the German eagle had its head facing towards a viewer's left, the Roman towards the right. When Charlemagne was made Kaiser of the empire he joined the two heads together, one looking east and one looking west. The golden eagle was also commemorative of the Crusades. In Norse legend it represents the wind, the form in which Odin, their chief god, flew with song mead to the realm of the gods. In Old Norse literature the eagle, raven and wolf were all beasts of battle who, when the fighting was over, ate their fill of the dead. In one of the Gudrum poems, the queen's brother says that the king lies slaughtered beyond the river, given to the wolves:

Look for Sigurd in the south.
There you will hear the ravens scream,

And the eagles scream exulting in their feast,
And the wolves howl over your husband.

Since earliest times the eagle has been depicted in art with the snake or a hare – the great and lofty triumphant over the lowly, light triumphant over darkness.

Because the eagle was considered to be the bird who could fly the highest, it was chosen by John Skelton (1460-1529) to oversee part of the funeral arrangements in his poem 'Philip Sparrow':

But for the eagle doth fly
Highest in the sky,
He shall be the sub-dean,
As provost principal,
To teach them their Ordinal.

Various accounts in European legends tell of the wren outwitting the eagle to be King of the Birds. Concealed in the eagle's feathers, the wren was carried high into the sky, flying off the back of the larger bird to take the title. Another story in a fifteenth-century manuscript has the birds competing to decide who can descend the furthest – the wren finds a mousehole!

William Shakespeare referred to the might of the eagle several times in his plays, such as in *Titus and Adronicus*:

The eagle suffers little birds to sing
And is not careful what they mean thereby;
Knowing, that with the shadow of his wings
He can at pleasure stint their melody.

According to *The Country-mans Counsellor* (1633) 'To dream of eagles flying over our heads foretells some of our Kinsfolk are departed'. Stones found in an eagle's nest were used as birth talismans. The Greeks and the Romans believed that the eagle had difficulty laying eggs and kept a stone to induce the right mood. A woman who had acquired such a stone was therefore assured of an easy childbirth.

FIELDFARE

. . . flocking fieldfares, speckled like the thrush,
Picking the red haw from the sweeing bush
That come and go on winter's chilling wing
And seem to share no sympathy with Spring.
March, Shepherd's Calendar, JOHN CLARE

FIELDFARE *(Turdus pilaris)*. The name fieldfare goes back to Middle English 'feldefare' and has been known as such since 1300. It literally means traveller over the fields. As a winter visitor it acquired names reflecting this status, such as snow bird, storm cock and storm bird while others refer to its slate-grey head and rump, such as blue bird, blue felt, grey thrush, blue tail and blue black. It is also known as fellfare, felfit, cock felt, hill bird and, from its cry, jack bird and screech bird. Fieldfares, who are inclined to be noisy and argumentative when they assemble in a flock looking for food, are traditionally looked upon as a winter visitor, although they actually start arriving in August. However, their numbers do increase dramatically in late October and they are among the last to depart in May. Nevertheless Lord De Talbley associated the bird with winter in his poem 'A Frosty Day':

When the fieldfare's flight is slow,
And a rosy vapour rim,
Now the sun is small and low,
Belts along the region dim.

According to the well known Yorkshire amateur weather forecaster William Fogget, it is a sign of bad weather to come when an unusually large flock of fieldfares arrives early. Although the birds are thought to have first nested here in Britain in the Orkneys in 1967, their numbers remain quite small. These elegant colourful members of the thrush family enjoy feeding in open countryside, descending in scattered flocks over farmland, open ground and gleaning in the stubble fields as befitting their name, seeking out worms and insects, always busily moving forward as they select their food source but constantly vigilant. If alarmed, they all take to the air and, having located a convenient tree, land, conspicuously facing into wind. Any further disturbance and away they go, flying down wind. In colder weather they enjoy the shelter and nature's treasures available in gardens and orchards – shrivelled fallen apples and the colourful berries of hawthorn, rowan and the larger rosehips of which Matthew Arnold wrote, using one of the bird's many regional names, 'scarlet berries gemmed, the fell-Fares' food'. His friend and walking companion of the glorious Lakeland countryside, William Wordsworth, also wrote of fell-fares. It is a bird of winter to Chaucer, in *The Parliament of Fowls*, a lengthy poem in which the Goddess of Nature presides over thirty-five birds, giving a brief description of each bird who has gathered on St Valentine's Day in order to choose a mate:

> *The raven wise; the crow with voice of care;*
> *The throstle old; the frosty fieldefare.*

Slightly smaller than the song thrush though more colourful it has a grey head, reddish-brown back, grey rump and black tail in contrast to the orange-buff breast and white belly. The fieldfare's nest of twigs and grasses is usually located in the fork of a tree, where five or six greenish-blue eggs are incubated.

The Romans had preserves of birds *(aviaria)* and apart from the usual pheasant, peacock and guinea fowl, the fieldfare was a favourite delicacy. Numerous birds were kept in large aviaries, and with the addition of ponds provided not only a source of food but also a considerable income for their owners. In Britain wild birds were caught with nets and a variety of traps and devices, some very cruel, were used. One trap, known as a pitfall, a pit slightly covered to entrap animals, was very popular and simple to construct. The word sweake, used in the following quotation from 'The Affectionate Shepherd' by Richard Barnfield, was part of such a trap which was usually baited.

Or in a misty morning, if thou wilt
Make pitfalls for the lark and fieldifare,
Thy prop and sweake shall be both over-gilt.

Lime-twigs, which are branches smeared with bird-lime – a viscous substance – held the bird fast, sticking to any part of the body it made contact with, most often the feet. An extract from the holly tree was a favourite substance.

I'll lend thee lime-twigs and sparrow calls,
Wherewith the fowler silly birds enthralls.

Fieldfare were thought to be insipid in flavour compared with other members of the thrush family such as the song and missel thrush and the redwing. Although cooked in a variety of ways, they were considered best spit-roasted, wrapped in a strip of larding bacon and served on a slice of bread fried in the cooking fat. They were also used as a substitute for thrush à la Bonne Femme. The trussed birds were cooked in butter in an earthenware casserole with small pieces of larding bacon and diced fried bread, and served sprinkled with brandy, game gravy and presented in the casserole. Small birds, potted, were also popular, having been previously boned and stuffed with foie gras and truffles.

GOLDFINCH

Sometimes goldfinches one by one will drop
From low-hung branches; little space they stop;
But sip, and twitter, and their feathers sleek;
Then off at once, as in a wanton freak:
Or perhaps, to show their black and golden wings
Pausing upon their yellow flutterings.
'I Stood Tip-toe Upon a Little Hill', JOHN KEATS

GOLDFINCH *(Carduelis carduelis)*. Goldfinch is a well known name going back to Old English 'goldfinc', suggesting the broad, golden wing bands seen in their full beauty when the bird is flying. The naturalist W Turner referred to gold finche in 1544, and by 1678 it was goldfinch or thistle-finch. Many regional names refer to the birds' rather exotic plumage, such as gold linnet, red-cap, seven-coloured linnet and lady with the twelve flounces. Eating habits are reflected in the Anglo-Saxon thisteltuige – thistle-tweaker, also thistle finch and thistle warp – thistles are their favourite plant food. And – from the birds' ability in a captive state to drink water by a cruel method from a small container – draw water. Brancher was a name used by London fanciers, referring to the one year old birds. The young birds were known generally as grey kates or grey pates, reflecting their dowdy head colour.

And when your little grey-pates
We'll help you to keep watch . . .
No prowling stranger cats shall come
About your high celestial home

wrote Sylvia Lynn in 'The Return of the Goldfinches'. In the same poem she touches on the craze for keeping caged wild goldfinches, which involved thousands of birds, reaching its peak in the latter half of the nineteenth century.

Believe me, birds, you need not fear,
No cages or limed twigs are here.

Ending this wretched practice was one of the main concerns of the Society for the Protection of Birds, later the Royal Society for the Protection of Birds. The Protection of Birds Act of 1880 technically gave the goldfinches protection. Two hundred years earlier William Shakespeare wrote of 'caged birds' whose 'notes of household harmony' gave pleasure but deprived them of their liberty. The poet William Cowper had two such birds, Tom and Dick, which he kept, caged, in his greenhouse – 'my summer seat'; In 'The Faithful Bird' he wrote of his pets:

They sang as blithe as finches sing
That flutter loose on golden wing,
And frolic where they list;
Strangers to liberty, 'tis true,
But that delight they never knew,
And therefore never missed.

Many types of trap were used to catch small birds. One in particular was the 'chardonneret' – the French name for the goldfinch. British law still allows the export of native finches bred in captivity, but it is illegal to trap or keep wild birds. In 1996 an estimated 10,000 birds were dispatched to Europe, of which nearly half were greenfinches. One hopes they do not share the fate of many of their kind as culinary delights, such as greenfinch tagliatelle or finch casserole. Other exports include goldfinches, bullfinches, linnets, chaffinches and siskins. The goldfinch is the most colourful and distinctive of all the British finches, with a striking plumage, a brown back with black wing feathers banded with brilliant yellow, and black tail feathers with pale tips similar to the wing feathers, and oval patches. A red face and black eye mask accentuate the pointed bill of this delicate feeder, who favours plants with interesting seedheads, such as thistles, hawkweeds, docks and teasels on which it performs great balancing feats, between acrobatic flutterings.

Aptly named collectively as a charm of goldfinch, these delightful birds build their nest rather high up towards the end of a tree branch. The fork of a tall apple tree is a favourite place, but prickly hedges of thorn or furze are also used, although there is always danger to contend with:

> *. . . the redcap too the while*
> *With gold freckd wings resumes his yearly toil*
> *And thoughtless were the thieving boys may come*
> *In the low eldern builds his dangerd home.*

The nest of the goldfinch is constructed with fine twigs, roots and grasses, delicately interwoven with moss and lichens and lined with wool, thistledown or hair. In May they lay four to six eggs, bluish in colour with some speckles.

It was not only the bright colourings of the goldfinch that attracted the attention of poets. Robert Burns, who referred to the bird as a 'gowdspink', was delighted by 'music's gayest child'. The familiar twittering night call and song is said to have a fluid quality. Michael Drayton compared it to that of the yellowhammer:

> *The yellow pate, which though she hurt the blooming tree*
> *Yet scarce hath any bird a finer pipe than she.*
> *And of these chanting fowls, the goldfinch not behind*
> *That hath so many sorts descending from her kind.*

A good omen was forecast for a girl seeing a goldfinch on St Valentine's Day – 'You will marry a desirable man'.

Heron

And herons, those grey stilted watchers,
From loch and corran rise,
And as they scream and squawk abuse
Echo from wooded cliff replies.
'The Brook', ALFRED, LORD TENNYSON

HERON *(Ardea cinera)*. Written references to the heron date back to the eighth century, though the word itself has its origin in Norman-French. The name hayroun occurs in 1300 and

shortly after came heyruns, both typical early references. The present spelling came into use in 1381 thereafter competing with hern, heronshaw and hernshaw, until 1768, when T Pennant, the ornithological expert, stated his preference – heron. The heron is a pre-Bronze Age bird with a wide variety of names, some referring to its cry, long neck or just a familiar name, such as Jack hern, Molly hern, Jemmy heron, Jemmy long-legs and tammie. Craigie heron (craig means throat), Frank hanser, diddleton Frank and Joan-na-ma-crank are from the harsh cry, whereas hernser, herald, hegrie, hernsew and hernshaw are regional names. Longie crane, long-necked heron, long neck longnix and lang-leggity beastie are self-explanatory.

> By him that hath the hern which by the fishy carr (pool)
> Can fetch with their long necks out of the rush and reed,
> Snigs, fry, and yellow frogs, whereon they often feed

wrote Michael Drayton in 'Polyolbion', touching on a favourite hunting ground of the heron. Ponds, lakes, rivers, marshes and other fresh water sites are the food territory of this expert fisherman. The heron with its large dagger-shaped bill and sharp eyesight has two fishing techniques, one is the unmistakable pose of the silent sentinel standing quite still, waiting for unsuspecting prey, and the other, quietly stalking on its elegant stilt-like legs with their spidery toes. Catching eels is one the heron's special accomplishments, as it grabs, not stabs, and swallows – our ancestors believed that the eel passed straight through its body. As eels were also the food of man it was thought that the heron must have some magical way of attracting them and other fish, possibly as it stood in the water; It was suggested that it was the fine grey powder in the bird's plumage sprinkled on its surface. Some thought to improve their catch by scattering pieces of the bird's legs in the water, while others carried a heron's foot in their pocket as a talisman.

The heron is an unmistakable and very distinguished-looking bird with a long neck and yellow bill, which turns pink during the breeding season. The unusual black and white plumage of the head, with down-swept crest, and fine long neck contrast with morning-coat grey and touches of black of the body. Herons tend to nest near water but some distance away from their fishing areas, and although some do nest on the ground they generally choose tall trees of ash, elm or oak, in which they lay four to five blue eggs. Large colonies form as unwieldy sticks are transformed into spacious nests. These constructions often become top-heavy as repairs are undertaken over the years. Formerly it was thought that the heron made holes in the bottom of the nest for their 'pig-squealing' young to pop their legs through. Ingenious but untrue, nevertheless accidents do happen in this high accommodation.

The heron from the ash's top
The eldest of its young lets drop,
As if it stork-like did pretend
That tribute to its lord to send

Herons were encouraged to nest 'by placing horse-head bones upon branches of tree' and could be induced to produce three clutches of four, then three and two successively in the year if the fledglings were removed.

Hawking for herons was a popular pastime, providing sport and food for the falconers. An anonymous fourteenth century poet graphically describes such an encounter in the long poem 'The Parliament of The Three Ages';

The hawks in the air hurtle down from on high,
And they hit the heron, whooped up by the falconers,
Buffet him, beat him, and bring him to the ground,
And assail him savegely and boldly seize him.
Then the falconers set out in hasty pursuit,
And run up hurriedly to give help to their hawks,
For with the bit of his bill the heron slashes about.
They drop down to their knees and crawl in cautiously,
Catch hold of his wings and wrench them together,
Burst open the bones and break them apart.
He picks out the marrow onto his glove with a quill,
And whoops them to the quarry that they crushed to death.

Sixteenth-century ornithologists claimed that the heron 'routs Eagles and Hawks, if they attack suddenly, by very liquid muting of the belly, and thereby defend itself'. Strange as it may seem, they did have a reputation for cowardice, as they tended to fly high and tried to avoid conflict with an adversary. Nevertheless Richard Lovelace (1618-1657) describes an encounter in, 'The Falcon', which refers to the fighting spirit of the heron when faced with an adversary – sometimes there are no winners.

> *The desp'rate heron now contracts*
> *In one design all former facts;*
> *Noble he is resolved to fall,*
> *His and his en'my's funeral.*

Falconry was a royal sport. The birds were kept in the mews at Charing Cross, from the reign of Richard II; however Henry VIII used the building for his horses. Herons must have been quite plentiful in the London area at that time, because the king issued a proclamation in an effort to preserve them in an area from his palace at Westminster to St Giles-in-the-Fields and from thence to Islington, Hampstead, Highgate and Hornsey Park.

In medieval Britain the variety of birds eaten was much greater than today. Herons, especially the young ones which at that time were known as heronshewes, were a popular dish in spring and summer and served in well-established households. At a feast there might be a choice of twenty dishes, which would include many wild birds. No banquet was complete without roast heron or crane (with which it was often confused) on the menu, although the former was considered lighter on the digestion. The Romans dealt with the problem of removing the sinews from the birds' neck by cooking them with their heads outside the water. When cooked they were wrapped in a warm cloth, and held tightly whilst the head was pulled off. In 1812 six birds were part of the fare in the Hall of the Stationers' Company in the City of London.

In folklore the heron is a symbol of fertility, forgetfulness,

longevity, morning, children and regeneration. It symbolizes morning because, standing in water or at the seashore, it is the first to welcome Dawn as she rises in the east – heron plumes are a symbol of silence.

In Angus, Scotland, a curious belief arose that the bird waxes and wanes with the phases of the moon. When the moon is full it is plump, and at the change it becomes so lean and feeble that it is unable to fly from a captor. In Ireland the bird's association with the planet required the heron to be killed at the full moon as its fat was considered a powerful specific for rheumatism. Weather-lorists regarded the heron flying up and down in the evening, as if doubtful where to rest, as a sign of bad weather. When a heron soars high, so as to fly above low cloud, it shows wind and when it flies low 'the air is gross and thickening into showers.'

> *When the shrill, screaming hern the ocean seeks,*
> *All these prognostics to the wise declare*
> *Pregnant with rain, though now serene, the air.*

A further sign of bad weather is:

> *When screaming to the land the lone hern flies,*
> *And from the crag reiterates her cries.*

And lastly a sign of wind:

> *When watchful herons leave their watery stand,*
> *And, mounting upward with erected flight,*
> *Gain on the skies, and soar above the sight.*

JACKDAW

There is a bird who, by his coat,
And by the hoarseness of his note,
Might be supposed a crow;
A great frequenter of the church,
Where, bishop-like, he finds a perch,
And dormitory too.
'The Jackdaw' WILLIAM COWPER

JACKDAW *(Corvus monedula)*. Until 1543 the common name of the bird was Jacke dawe which was abbreviated to Jack-daw (or) chough by the natural history authority C Merret in 1667. However from 1768, jackdaw became the standard word, generally reflecting its familiar chattering call. Local names based on the cry are caw, caddaw, carder, jakie cawdaw and coe. However, James Thomson in his poem, 'The Seasons (Spring)' uses another name, daw, including other members of the gregarious crow family;

> *The jay, the rook, the daw,*
> *And each harsh pipe, discordant heard alone,*
> *Aid the full concert.*

During the sixteenth century the word daw also meant knave or someone held in low esteem. It was in this context that William Shakespeare in Henry VI referred to the bird:

> *Between two hawks, which flies the higher pitch;*
> *Between two dogs, which hath the deeper mouth,*
> *Between two blades, which bears the better temper,*
> *Between two horses, which doth bear him best;*
> *Between two girls, which hath the merriest eye;*
> *I have perhaps some shallow spirit of judgement;*
> *But in these nice sharp quillets of the law,*

Good faith, I am no wiser than a daw.

Other names such as grey head, grey pate and pate refer to the bird's plumage, particularly the ash-grey sides of the neck, nape and the back of the head, which blend with the black wings, tail and knee breeches.

. . . greybeard jackdaws, noising as they fly,

wrote John Clare in 'Autumn Birds'.

Jackdaws are generally widespread throughout Britain and are seen on farmland, in woodland, on sea cliffs, and in towns and cities. They breed in loose colonies, often using the same nest site each year. The jackdaw considers a chimney a welcome substitute for a tree, where it haphazardly drops a variety of sticks until one forms the main spar and so the nest progresses. It is therefore not surprising that jackdaws occasionally fell down the chimney, which was believed to foretell a death in the family. They also build or perhaps one should say pile their sticks up in large crevices in rocks or holes, old trees, even a rabbit burrow is acceptable. Their eggs, four to six in number, are blue-green in colour.

In folklore the jackdaw signifies empty conceit, vain assumption, also imitativeness, inasmuch as it can be trained to imitate human speech. In several parts of England the sight of a jackdaw by a bride-to-be on her way to the church was thought to signify her marriage would be happy and prosperous. Many believed that a solitary jackdaw was a sign of death. Others merely regarded the bird as a sign of rain, as suggested by the East Anglian rhyme:

> *When three daws are seen on St Peter's vane together*
> *Then we are sure to have bad weather.*

Evidence that the bird was thought to be unlucky is recorded in *Brand's Observations on Popular Antiquities* (1877): 'In the time of Charles VIII of France the battle that was fought between the French and Brittans in which Brittans were overthrown, was foreshewed by a skirmish between Magpies and Jackdaws.'

Perhaps the most famous legend associated with the bird is 'The Jackdaw of Rheims', written by an English clergyman, Richard Harris Barham. He wrote many comic tales and verse, but in this long amusing poem he exposed superstitious practises within the church. The opening verse sets the scene for the theft of the cardinal's ring.

> *The Jackdaw sat on the Cardinal's chair,*
> *Bishop and abbot and prior were there;*
> *Many a knight and many a squire,*
> *With a great many more of lesser degree –*
> *. . . the great Cardinal sat*
> *In the great Lord Cardinal's great red hat;*
> *And he peered in the face of his Lordship's Grace*
> *With a satisfied look, as if he would say,*
> *'We are the greatest folks here today.'*

The stolen ring was eventually found in the nest of the jackdaw who 'got plenary absolution' and in the natural course of time:

> *It's the custom at Rome new names to bestow*
> *So they canonised him by the name of Jim Crow!*

J AY

For 'tis the mind that
*   makes the body rich:*
And as the sun breaks
*   through the darkest clouds,*
So honour peereth in the meanest
*   habit.*
What, is the jay more precious than the
lark
Because his feathers are more beautiful?
The Taming of the Shrew, WILLIAM SHAKESPEARE

JAY *(Garrulus glandarius)*. The name jay came to us through the Normans. It presupposes Old French jai, modern French is geai. The name jay was established by 1310, replacing the Old English ' higera' or 'higora', as the riddle, possibly eighth century, suggests:

> *I am a wonder. I vary my voice,*
> *Sometimes I bark like a dog, sometimes bleat like a goat*
> *Sometimes I honk like a goose, sometimes shriek like a hawk.*
> *Sometimes I mimic the dusty eagle,*
> *That war-bird's cry, sometimes I mock*
> *The kite's voice, sometimes the gull singing*
> *Where I sit glad. G suggests me,*
> *Also A and R, with O,*
> *H and I. Now I am named,*
> *As these six letters clearly say.*

The Gaelic name for the jay, *Schreachag choille* – screamer of the woods – seems particularly apt. Chaucer speaks of 'the scorning jay' in *The Parliament of Fowls*, whilst Michael Drayton preferred 'the counterfeiting jay' in 'The Muses

Elysium'. Other local names include gae, blue jay, jay pie, jay piet, jenny jay, kae, devil scritch, scold and oak jackdaw.

The jay can be seen in deciduous and conifer woods, wooded farmland, parks and gardens with plenty of trees and bushes.The nest is usually low down in dense cover and well hidden, consisting of sticks and twigs interlaced to form a deep bowl and lined with rootlets and sometimes horsehair, although John Clare saw an alternative lining:

> *... yonder by the circling stack*
> *Provoking any eye to smile*
> *A pye perched on the heifer's back*
> *Pulls hair to line her nest the while.*

Incubation of the greenish-brown eggs with delicate markings is shared, as is the nest building, by both parents.

This raucous member of the crow family which, with the exception of the magpie, is black, is a very attractive bird with pinkish-brown upper body and a lighter shaded breast, a pleasing contrast to the white rump and long black tail feathers. It has a distinctive whitish crown streaked black which forms a small crest, when erect.

> *The jay set up his copple crown*
> *And screamed to see a stranger*
> *And swopt and hurried up and down*
> *To warn the birds of danger,*

wrote John Clare. A drooping black moustache adds a comical touch above the white patch below the beak. The black wing feathers have a bright, white panel and a black barred patch of blue which Thomas Gisborne describes perfectly, in 'Walks In A Forest':

> *... proud of cerulean stains*
> *From heaven's unsullied arch purloined, the jay*
> *Screams hoarse.*

John Masefield is less flattering with his 'blue winged Judas' Nevertheless one is more likely to hear a jay than see one,

although they are frequently seen at dawn, when fewer people are stirring. They have a marked preference for acorns and can often be seen dropping down to the ground from the lower branches of an oak tree. Rooks and jays have a distendable pouch in which to collect nuts, burying thousands each year as potential food supplies, many of which remain uncollected but contribute to the regeneration of oak trees. However this is small consolation for their reputation as egg thieves and killers of fledglings.

Jays were persecuted by gamekeepers during the last century and often formed part of the display gibbet favoured by the men of the moleskin vest:

> *With pockets deep and wide*
> *And many are the birds and beasts*
> *That find their way inside.*
> *A sparrow-hawk, an owl, a stoat,*
> *A weasel, and a jay –*
> *To keep the pheasants free from harm*
> *So much there is to slay!*

wrote E V Lucas in 'The Gamekeeper'.

The jay was regarded as a great delicacy when young. However the fully grown birds could be eaten but had to be boiled before roasting – acccording to *Larrousse Gasronomique*.

KESTREL

I caught this morning morning's minion, kingdom
of daylight's dauphin, dapple-dawn-drawn falcon, in his
riding
Of the rolling level underneath him steady air, and striding
High there, how he rung upon the rein of a wimpling wing
In his ecstasy! then off, off forth on swing,
As a skate's heel sweeps smooth on a bow-bend: the hurl and
gliding
Rebuffed the big wind.
'The Windhover', GERARD MANLEY HOPKINS

KESTREL *(Falco tinnunculus)*. The name kestrel came to us via the Normans from the Old French crecele; the modern word is *crecerelle*, meaning rattle, which is probably imitative of the bird's courtship call, 'kee-kee-kee'. Nevertheless the bird has managed to collect a variety of local names too numerous to list, including many that not only reflect its amazing ability to hover, but also the bloodthirsty family business of hunting. They include the descriptive windhover, hoverhawk, wind cutter, wind fanner, stand hawk, stannel, stonegall, red hawk, mouse hawk and blood hawk. The kestrel is the most widespread bird of prey in England and can be seen in many places, including city centres. At the turn of the century it was the commonest bird of prey in London, where it can be found today surviving on a diet of sparrows and the occasional pigeon. In the mid-sixties the wildlife artist James Alder wrote in the *Evening Chronicle* of a kestrel's nest on a huge tower crane in a famous shipyard. The birds had evicted the previous occupants, a pair of breeding rooks, from the nest which was constructed mainly of wire. According to his article, 'The hen-kestrel was sitting her eggs fairly tightly and it was possible to

walk along the cat-
walk within eight
feet of her
before she left
her nest, when
she would fly
around the
crane and
swoop at me
to scare me
away.' Happily
they survived.
Miles of road-
side verges
bounded by
hedgerows and
trees, as well as central
reservations, are
favourite hunting grounds.
The birds not only provide interest, but also an awareness of wild life to
passing motorists and a permanent surprise to voles and mice
who inhabit these undisturbed areas. Searching the grass for a
meal,

> *An ever-watchful eye supported on vibrating wings;*
> *No movement evades it,*
> *Elegant but deadly*

wrote John Savage as an observant fourteen-year-old young
ornithologist. Kestrels enjoy the freedom of open country and
like all birds of prey have excellent eyesight.

> *Up on the downs the red-eyed kestrels hover,*
> *Eyeing the grass,*
> *The field-mouse flits like a shadow into cover*
> *As their shadows pass.*

The handsome, trim male bird has a chestnut-brown back and

long pointed wing feathers spotted black, with a blue head sporting a rakish black moustache. The silvery blue tail has a conspicious black band. Although the female has chestnut colouring she is much duller with darker brown barring on her tail. Courtship displays in the spring involve the male diving at the female, uttering a shrill scream either when she is perched or flying. If the latter she presents her talons to him. Kestrels nest in the holes of trees, crevices in a cliff face or a wall, abandoned nests of other species or on ledges in old buildings. Nest hardly describes what is merely a scrape of debris with no real nesting material. Nevertheless four or five white eggs with reddish-brown markings are duly incubated by the female. Unfortunately a number of chicks are stolen each year from various nest sites by human predators. Although these would-be falconers may attempt to train and fly the birds, many are abandoned to their inevitable fate, Fortunately the trapping of birds has declined in recent years except where a licence has been granted. Before Parliamentary legislation introduced a ban on pole traps in Britain they were used extensively by gamekeepers to control kestrels, sparrowhawks and crows.

In the earlier history of falconry the kestrel was assigned to a knave, and as it was considered to be a hawk of base breed it was likened to a worthless man, as Edmund Spenser implies in the *Faerie Queene*:

> *No thought of honour ever did assay*
> *His baser brest; but in his kestrell kynd*
> *A pleasant veine of glory he did find . . .*

According to Lipton in *A Thousand Notable Things* there is rivalry amongst some birds of prey: 'The Sparrowhawk is a fierce enemy to all pigeons; but they are defended by the castre (Kestrel or Standhawk) whose sight and voice the Sparrowhawk doth fear . . . which pigeons know well enough, for where the castrel is, from thence will not pigeons go (if the Sparrowhawk be nigh) through the great trust she hath in her defender.'

KINGFISHER

It was the Rainbow gave thee birth,
And left thee all her lovely hues;
And, as her mother's name was Tears,
So runs it in thy blood to choose
For haunts the lonely pools . . .
'The Kingfisher', W H DAVIES

KINGFISHER *(Alcedo atthis)*. Formerly king's fisher, however, the oldest known name for this bird is found in Old English 'isen', 'isern', said to be Germanic in origin, meaning iron-coloured, i.e. blue. An earlier name 'iscere', although not recorded during the Middle English period, lives on in fisher. The present name, kingfisher, interpreted as excellent fisherman, appeared in about 1658, although preceded in 1318 by king's fisher. Joshua Sylvester (1563-1618) wrote:

And the kings-fisher, which so builds her nest
By the seaside in midst of winter season . . .

Nevertheless there is a distinct short-
age of local names. One, dipper,
which also applies to other
birds, simply indicates a
bird who dives into
water after fish.

The first impres-
sion of those that
have the good for-
tune to catch a
glimpse of what must
be Britain's most
exotic-looking bird, is

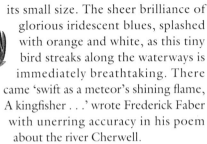

its small size. The sheer brilliance of glorious iridescent blues, splashed with orange and white, as this tiny bird streaks along the waterways is immediately breathtaking. There came 'swift as a meteor's shining flame, A kingfisher . . .' wrote Frederick Faber with unerring accuracy in his poem about the river Cherwell.

These highly territorial birds are particularly vocal in spring and autumn when they are establishing breeding and wintering territories on banks and coastal strips. The parent birds share the nest building by tunnelling out their nest hole – in which five or six white rounded eggs are laid – with their powerful bills. As they have rather disgusting nesting habits the scrape soon piles up with scales, fishbones and regurgitated pellets. Their habit of plunging headlong into the water when they leave the nest cleanses their splendid plumage. The nature poet John Clare watched them fishing in Northamptonshire:

> *In coat of orange green and blue*
> *Now on a willow branch I view*
> *Grey waving to the sunny gleam*
> *King fishers watch the ripple stream*
> *For little fish that nimble bye*
> *And in the gravel shallows lie.*

Perched like sentinels on overhead branches, they catch fish half their body weight. As part of the mating ritual the male will often present one to his partner.

In Greek mythology the kingfisher is dedicated to Thetis, an ocean nymph. The bird was said to lay eggs in a nest of fishbones on the sea during the winter solstice, where they were incubated by the hen for fourteen days. During this time the water remained placid:

So long as there her quiet couch she keeps,
Sicilian sea exceeding calmly sleeps

Halcyon Days are the fourteen days; a time of happiness and prosperity. Halcyon is another name for the kingfisher, from *hals*, sea and *kuo*, to brood on. Another Greek legend suggests the kingfisher is dedicated to Zeus who sent a thunderbolt, destroying the ship in which Ceyx, husband of Alcyone, the moon goddess who protected seafarers from the storms, was sailing. In her anguish Alcyone threw herself into the sea, and with her love, was changed by Thetis into a kingfisher.

Superstition held that the dried body of the kingfisher would ward off lightning. In Britain our ancestors had an unlikely use for the carcass too, as it was recommended as a moth deterrent, giving off 'a pleasant odour to clothes'. One writer advises that when the bird is hung by a thread from the ceiling it will always turn its beak to whatever the direction of the wind blew. In Wild's *Iter Boreale* an alternative weather omen suggests that:

> *The peaceful KING-FISHERS are met together*
> *About the decks, and prophesie calm weather.*

A further sign of fine weather is when:

> *The stars shine smarter; and the moon adorns,*
> *As with borrowed beams, her sharpened horns;*
> *The filmy gossamer now flits no more,*
> *Nor halcyons bask on the short sunny shore.*

A charming story accounting for the colour of the bird's feathers relates that the dove and the kingfisher were sent from Noah's Ark in search of dry land. Because the kingfisher flew so high its plumage was stained with the brilliant colours of the sun and sky.

L APWING

They alone move, now low, now high,
And merrily they cry
To the mischievous Spring sky,
Plunging earthward, tossing high,
Over the ghost who wonders why
So merrily they cry and fly,
Nor choose 'twixt earth and sky
EDWARD THOMAS 'Two Pewits'.

LAPWING *(Vanellus vanellus)*. The name lapwing has its roots in the eighth and nineth century with variations on laepiewince. The first part was believed to be the name of a bird in its own right, and wince meaning one that turns. Despite various etymological distortions, by the sixxteenth century, lapwing was in general use. The bird is also known as green plover, peewit, peesweep, horneywink, old maid, lapwingle, lappin, flopwing, teuchit, tuwet and plover, amongst others, plus regional variations. The name peewit and peesweep reflect the persistant, haunting, wailing call of the bird for which various legendary explanations are given;

In the Christian tradition, a handmaiden of the the Virgin Mary is alleged to have stolen one of her mistress's dresses, for which reason she was turned into a lapwing, forever condemned to cry: 'Tyvit,Tyvit',; (I stole it, I stole it). Another story has the bird mocking Christ at the crucifixion, condemned everafter to live homeless, calling soulfully. An historical connection was made with the Lincolnshire family of Tyrwhitts when a man fell wounded and was only rescued because of the alarming cry of the bird.

From *Leydens Glossary to the Complaynt* of Scotland (1801)

'thuesnek' (the cry of the lapwing), 'though not reckoned ominous, this bird is detested in the south and west of Scotland, on the ground that, the solitary haunts of the lapwing being frequently invaded by Prestbyterian fugitives from cruel persecution to which they were subjected to in the reign of Charles, James II, its clamours at their intrusion revealed their retreat.' In eastern Scotland its spring return is said to coincide with the last blast of winter and for this reason it is called the teuchat storm.

Apart from the high mountains and uplands lapwings are widely distributed throughout Britain. Forming loose flocks (the collective noun for the birds is a conceit of lapwing) they can be found on grassland and ploughed fields, mainly in the winter. In summer, they prefer moorland and wet meadows and, in spring, cultivated land. The nest is just a scrape on dry land with an apology of a lining – wisps of grass, straw or heather – in which they lay three to five, sharply pointed dusky, stone brown-splotched eggs. This gregarious medium sized wading bird has a most elegant upward-curling crest which is set off by a wide black half-collar, white under vest and dark bronze-green back and wing feathers. The crest was the subject of an obscure old riddle:

> *What is up when it is down*
> *And down when it is up?*

In Celtic mythology the lapwing is the animal of Bran, the underworld ruler. Its poetic meaning as understood by the Bards was to disguise the secret; the dog to guard the secret and the roebuck was to hide the secret.

In folklore lapwing signifies deceit and artfulness.

The eggs of the lapwing were formerly considered to be an unrivalled delicacy and sold in great numbers to London shops. Egg collecting was a well established trade. In spring shepherds trained their dogs to hunt for the nests, a welcome supplement to their meagre income. Nevertheless the female bird used to try and mislead her hunters by flapping along the ground as though she was lame, with her partner wheeling round and making a clamorous noise over the heads of the intruders.

> *And many lapwings cried pee-wit;*
> *And one among the rest*
> *Pretended lameness to decoy*
> *Us from her lonely nest*

wrote Adelaide O'Keeffe in 'Eyes and No eyes'. Earlier writers noticed these antics as an old English proverb indicates: 'The lapwing cries most, farthest from her nest'.

The birds were said to be easily tamed and often kept in gardens 'where they were said to do much good by destroying the slugs and worms on which they feed'.

> *The pewet hollos chewsit as she flyes*
> *And flops about the shepherd where he lies*
> *But when her nest is found she stops her song*
> *And cocks her coppled crown and runs along*

observed John Clare. Formerly it was believed that the lapwing chicks left the nest almost as soon as they had hatched, as they were sometimes seen with pieces of shell on their heads – which in fact was often due to being disturbed – nevertheless any strange behaviour was likened to this oddity. William Shakespeare in *Hamlet* has Horatio saying of the foolish Osric 'the lapwing runs with shell on his head'.

In kitchens throughout the land lapwing eggs were boiled hard and served hot or cold. For breakfast, a basket lined with moss was considered to be the ideal ornament for the table – otherwise a folded napkin. Peeled eggs piled in the centre of a dish, surrounded by a ring of aspic jelly, were recommended as

a fashionable dish for luncheons or suppers. Bird wholesalers explained that lapwings were of no use after an early date in the year 'after they have begun to lap'.

O, lapwing, thou fliest around the heath,
Nor seest the net that is spread beneath.
Why dost thou not fly among the corn fields?
They cannot spread nets where a harvest yields

wrote William Blake(1757-1827). But danger lurked in the air too:

He lifts the tube, and levels with his eye;
Straight a short thunder breaks the frozen sky:
Oft, as in airy rings they skim the heath,
The clam'rous lapwings feel the leaden death.

Lapwings were eaten from the beginning of September to the end of January but deemed scarcely fit for anything but roasting; nevertheless they were also stewed or made into a ragout but this method of cooking was not recommended. Mrs Beeton, in her *Everyday Cookery Book*, advised that after the birds had been plucked but not drawn, were wiped clean with a damp cloth and trussed with the head under the wing 'put them down to a clear fire, and lay slices of moistened toast in the dripping pan to catch the trail. Keep them well basted, dredge lightly with flour. Dish them on toasts, over which the trail should be equally spread. Pour round the toast a little good gravy'.

LINNET

LINNET *(Carduelis cannabina)*. Linnet is from the Old French, *linette*, and has been known by that name since the thirteenth century consisting of lin, flax, from Latin *linum* and the diminutive suffix ette, which is comparable to our English ling. By 1530 linnet was the established word. The bird has numerous local names which either refer to its habitat or winter and summer plumage. The colourful crimson-red crown and breast patches of the male bird are reflected in red linnet, rose linnet, red-headed finch and red-breasted linnet. In winter the colour of the plumage of female and male alike is suggested in grey linnet, whin grey, brown linnet or simply grey bird. Finally while the habitat for this early spring nesting bird is revealed in furze or gorse linnet, whin linnet, gorse hatcher, gorse bird and thorn linnet. Scottish names include lintie and lint white.

In spite of a serious decline in their population during the nineteenth century the linnet is now widespread throughout Britain. Although it is often associated with gorse on moorland and heath it can be seen in open country too. Nevertheless as they often start nesting before other shrubs are in leaf, gorse does provide year round cover and prickly security from predators. The linnet tends to nest near the top of a bush or hedge and, if you bend down, it can often be seen silhouetted against the light. These sociable birds prefer to nest in groups; as many as forty pairs are said to have been counted within an area of two hectares. A delightful description of the nest and the incubation of the linnet's eggs is given by Erasmus Darwin in 'The Temple of Nature':

Soft thistle-down, grey moss, and scattered wool,
Line the secluded nest with feathery rings,
Meet with fond bills, and woo fluttering wings.
Week after week, regardless of her food,
The incumbent linnet warms her future brood
Each spotted egg with ivory lips she turns,
Day after day with fond expectance burns,
Hears the young prisoner chirping in his cell
And breaks in hemispheres the obdurate shell.

In winter they form lively flocks assembling at dusk, singing and performing aerial displays, bouncing and circling in undulating flight for some time before settling down with a certain amount of discord over perching positions. During the day, as Robert Bridges recalls in his poem 'Spring':

Linnets and twites, in small flocks helter-skelter,
All the afternoon to the gardens fly
From thistle-pastures hurrying to gain the shelter
Of American rhododendron or cherry-laurel.

The elegance and song of the male bird is particularly noticeable during the breeding season when it perches openly, which is unusual for this inconspicuous species:

> *I heard a linnet courting*
> *His lady in the spring;*
> *His mates were idly sporting,*
> *Nor stayed to hear him sing*
> *His song of love.*

wrote Robert Bridges. The colourful plumage of the linnet, and the beauty of its tinkling song, contributed to the earlier decline in numbers. It attracted the attention of bird catchers who used festoons of limed twigs on trees and bushes to attract them. They waited quietly nearby, leaping out to seize the birds as quickly as possible, as they struggled to free themselves from the glutinous substance without damaging the plumage. One cruel practice of the time was to sear the eyes of wild birds with a red hot wire or needle in order to make them sing. The place where song birds could be bought was alleged to be Stupidity Street which, if true, is aptly named:

> *I saw with open eyes*
> *Singing birds sweet*
> *Sold in the shops*
> *For the people to eat,*
> *Sold in the shops of*
> *Stupidity Street*

wrote Ralph Hodgson in a poem of that name.

In the poem 'Who killed Cock Robin'? the linnet carries the link – torch:

> *Who'll carry the link?*
> *I, said the linnet,*
> *I'll fetch it in a minute,*
> *I'll carry the link.*

MAGPIE

I wondered where and from whom the pie could have learned
To put together the sticks in which she lays and broods,
For there is no craftsman, I know, who could construct her nest,
And it would be a wonder if any mason had made such a
mould.
'Piers Plowman', WILLIAM LANGLAND

MAGPIE *(Pica pica)*. Pie is the ultimate source of most of the numerous English names for the magpie, borrowed from the French pie and derived from Latin pica. The name magpie must be older than one of the earliest traceable references in 1605 'as merrie as a magge pie'. However regional variations and spelling provide a diversity of names for this sartorially elegant member of the crow family. Although reputed to be no mean collector, the magpie's other names include such favourites as mock-a-pie, nanpie, longtailed nan, pianate and chatterpie. William Shakespeare favoured, in his Scottish play *Macbeth*, magot pie:

Augurs and understood relations
have,
By magot-pies, and choughs
and rooks, brought forth
The secret'st man of blood

As the first syllable of magpie is diminutive form of Margaret, mag, madge, miggy and Margaret's pie, with additional per-mutations, were also popular.

The magpie was often persecuted in areas where game is reared, frequently being strung out, gibbet style, on fences and trees with other birds and small animals.

> *Though on your long-tailed flight,*
> *You wore half-mourning of staid black and white,*
> *So little did the thought of death*
> *Enter your thievish head*
> *You never knew what choked your breath*
> *When in a day turned night*
> *You fell with feathers heavier than lead*

wrote Andrew Young in 'A Shot Magpie'.

The magpie prefers grassland bounded with thick hedges and trees. They are found on farmland too, and increasingly seen in gardens and parks feeding on invertebrates in the summer and, later in the year, seeds and berries. Chattering groups assemble in the winter circling around the tree branches, call-ing and displaying in an excitable manner, conspicuous in their distinctive black and white livery – formerly bishops were humorously called magpies - blue wing feathers and iridescent green tail with its reddish-purple tip. Both partners construct their domed-shaped nests of twigs – thorny ones for the roof,lined with earth, fine roots and grass – into which are laid five or six greenish-blue eggs – with speckled dark markings.

John Clare kept a magpie which learned to talk: 'I kept one for years till it got drowned in a well it used to see itself in the water I fancy it got down thinking to meet itself it used to run away with teaspoons or anything it could,' he wrote of his unusual thieving companion. In folklore the magpie symbol-izes garrulity, mischievousness and noisiness and is sacred to Bacchus, Greek and Roman god of fertility and wine.

In Europe during the Middle Ages the chattering of a mag-pie in a tree indicated the visit of a stranger. This was not neces-sarily a good omen, as the bird was said to be tainted with a drop of the devil's blood. There were those who, on sighting a magpie with its swaggering legionnaire's gait, would take off their hat and spit in the direction of the bird, saying 'Devil, devil, I defy you'. Nevertheless a more conciliatory tone was preferred by others who would merely doff their hat and say 'Good morrow, Mr Magpie, how are you today?' The more cautious added an enquiry on the health of Mrs Magpie. Crossing oneself was also thought to prevent any evil effects, as an old rhyme suggests:

> *The magpie crosses me*
> *Bad luck to the magpie*
> *Good luck to me.*

For those who felt the need of protection from above:

> *I crossed the pynot*
> *And the pynot crossed me,*
> *The devil take the pynot,*
> *And God save me.*

There were those who simply turned around in another direction so that bad luck did not cross their path. However the sight of a crow soon afterwards was said to mitigate any possible ill effect. The magpie has long been regarded as a bird of prophecy and there are many variations on the following rhyme:

> *One for anger, two for mirth,*
> *Three for a wedding, and four for a*
> *   birth,*
> *Five for silver, six for gold,*
> *Seven for a secret that shall never*
> *   be told.*

An alternative rhyme retaining the first two lines:

> *Five for rich, six for poor,*
> *Seven for a bitch, eight for a*
> *   whore,*

Nine for a burying, ten for a dance,
Eleven for England, twelve for France.

Or:

One is a sign of mischief, two is a sign of mirth,
Three is a sign of a wedding, four is a sign of death,
Five is a sign of rain, six is the sign of a bastard bairn.

And on a lighter note:

Round about, round about,
Maggoty pie;
My father loves good ale,
And so do I.

According to country lore two magpies chattering in their distinctive machine-gun cackle in the garden of a married couple indicates a violent quarrel. Which in no way justifies the collective noun for the birds – a murder of magpies. In total contrast three or four magpies together, making harsh cries, predict windy weather. When the weather is warm they will leave their nest unattended, but if it is cold and stormy one will stay behind. As a result anglers regarded the sight of one magpie as an unfavourable omen.

Although the mature bird was not generally regarded as palatable, as the flesh was said to be very dry, it was used in kitchens for making stock. However the young birds, being tender, were quite acceptable, roasted. In folk medicine it was believed that eating a mixture of ground-up magpie could cure epilepsy, on the basis that a chatterer could neutralize a chattering disease.

M OORHEN

And near unpeopled stream-sides, on the ground,
By her spring-cry the moor-hen's nest is found,
Where the drained flood-lands flaunt their marigold.
'Spring', D G ROSSETTI

MOORHEN *(Gallinula chloropus)*. Gallinula literally means chicken, a diminutive of *gallina*, hen, derived from gallus, cock. Common gallinule (water chicken) was up to this century in fairly general use in bird books, although it is now a generic name for various exotic species. From 1300 the bird was documented as mor-hen, then in 1655 as moor hen and by 1678 water-hen or more-hen; The word 'moor' suggesting the old meaning – marsh. Water hen remains the popular form today. Other names include moorcock, mere hen, stank hen, water rail, mor coot, kitty coot and cuddy.

Moorhens have conspicuous white V-shaped flashes under their short black rounded tail feathers, which they flick at the slightest sign of danger or a territorial dispute. During the mating season, both male and female raise and flirt their

tails displaying the soft white under-feathers. If display alone fails to resolve any local difficulties, their yellow-tipped red bill comes into play and they will fight noisily and vigorously, assisted by their red-gartered, long greenish-coloured legs, with splendidly adapted long toes which are ideal for a hasty retreat across marshy ground, floating debris or waterlily leaves. They are very adaptable without the assistance of the usual webbed toes, and are capable of staying under water by clasping on to the vegetation, often leaving their bill, like a miniature periscope, poking out above the surface, as recommended in all survival manuals! The moorhen is sometimes confused with the coot, who has a similar habitat but is larger and has a different white marking:

> And in old scatter'd pits, the flags and reeds beneath,
> The coot, bald, else clean black, that whiteness it doth bear
> Upon the forehead starred, the water-hen doth wear
> Upon her little tail in one small feather set

wrote Michael Drayton, slightly understating the white feathers. Although they are usually associated with water, moorhens do forage on grassland and regularly roost in trees, often building their nests there, too. Otherwise they nest under the cover of waterside bushes, or the overhanging branches and floating heaps of waterweeds of fresh water pools, lakes and streams. When the moorhen takes off from the water it patters along the surface, eventually trailing its legs in flight. Each year they return to their old nesting sites, as John Clare observed in 'The Moorhen's Nest':

> And once again a couple from the brood
> Seek their old birth place – and in safetys mood
> Lodge there their flags and lay though danger comes
> It dares and tries and cannot reach their homes
> And so they hatch their eggs and sweetly dream
> On their shelfed nests that bridge the gulphy stream.

Two or three broods are reared each year, the moorhen laying between five and eleven eggs – a glossy buff colour with brown and black blotches. The new brood are a joy to watch (a child-hood memory) small black downy bundles with minute orange-red bills, flapping their tiny wings in the air to attract attention, as they get on with the business of living. As soon as possible after hatching they follow the parent into the water. Several broods each season ensures the survival of the moorhen as the chicks become the prey of marauding pikes and water rats.

And soon the sutty brood from fear elopes
Where bulrush forrests give them sweeter hopes
Their hanging nests that aids their wishes well
Each leaves for water as it leaves the shell
And dive and dare and every gambol try.
Till they themselves to other scenes can fly

continued John Clare.

The position of the nests was seen as a means of weather divination. Should the moorhen build its nest high up on the banks of ponds or in bushes it will be a wet summer; if close by the water, it will be dry.

Moorhens have been snared for centuries and, like the coot, classified by the Church as Lenten fare. However because of their habitat and diet they were said to have a 'muddy' flavour when cooked. Although the moorhen, eaten fresh, could be skinned and roasted, a sharp knife was more often used to cut away the unpalatable skin and remove the breast, which many considered to be the only edible part of the bird. The dark flesh, which is rather dry and not strongly flavoured, was rec-ommended with larding bacon, as suitable for a casserole.

NIGHTINGALE

Hark! that's the nightingale,
Telling the selfsame tale
Her song told when this ancient earth was young:
So echoes answered when her song was sung
In the first wooded vale.
'Pain or Joy', CHRISTINA ROSSETTI

NIGHTINGALE *(Luscinia megarhynchos)*. The common name is from Old English 'nihtegale' and continues into Middle English, to be last recorded in 1483 as 'nyghtgale'. A variant nihtingale appeared in the middle of the thirteenth century, and is the source of the modern word. Older European variants suggest the word literally means songstress. The Latin name *luscinia* is from *luctus* – lamentation – and cano – sing. The Old English version comes from 'nihte', night, and 'gale' – singer. The only other name for the nightingale seems to be an East Anglian one – barley bird, which may have some connection with the spring sowing of the seed and the appearance of the bird, which is also linked with the cuckoo in a traditional oral saying:

> *On the third of April*
> *Come the Cuckoo and the Nightingale*

The two birds are also associated in the omen that if you should hear a nightingale sing before the cuckoo this is a lucky sign that your love affair will run smoothly. If by chance your sweetheart should be with you, then clasp hands and stand quite still in silence while you count to thirty, and your love will end in marriage.

Philomel is a poetical name for the nightingale which appears in numerous poems expressing sorrow, forlorn love or

simply the beauty of its song.

Sing'st thou, sweet Philomel, to me,
For that I also long
Have practised in the groves like thee,
Though not like thee in song?

wrote William Cowper in 'To The Nightingale', after hearing
the bird singing one New Year's Day. Philomela, which literally
means love of song was, in Greek mythology, the name of the
daughter of an Athenian king; and the the sister of Procne,
whose husband the Thracian king, Tereus, ravished Philomela,
then cut off her tongue so that she would not reveal this terrible deed to his wife. Tereus told his wife that Philomela was
dead, but in the meantime she carefully embroiderd the story
of her fate into a tapestry and sent it to Procne. Philip Sidney
in his 'Nightingale' poem, regarded this more as impetuous
ardour:

Alas!, she hath no other cause for anguish
But Tereus' love, on her by strong hand wroken.

Nevertheless the reunited sisters exacted a terrible revenge by
killing Itys, son of Tereus, serving the flesh to his father. Tereus
discovered what the sisters had done and he was about to kill
them when the gods intervened, changing Procne into a swallow, Philomela a nightingale and Tereus into a hoopoe.

Matthew Arnold refers to the tragedy in 'Philomela':

> *O wanderer from a Grecian shore,*
> *Still, after many years, in distant lands,*
> *Still nourishing in thy bewilder'd brain*
> *That wild unquench'd deep-sunken, old-world pain.*

In folklore the nightingale symbolizes happiness and sweetness, as well as a bad omen, forlornness and unrequited love.

On the bird's return in mid-April from the Sahara it can be seen in woodland, mainly in the south of England, singing a variety of rich notes and phrases night and day – contrary to popular belief. This rare bird particularly favours dense thickets of overgrown coppice woodland where they nest close to the ground amongst vegetation. With much hopping and twitching of tail and wings they make a nest of leaves lined with grass and hair, in which four or five bluish-green eggs, heavily speckled, are laid. Their plumage of rich warm brown upper parts, creamy buff under-parts and rather long chestnut-shaded tail, provide the perfect camouflage for these groundfeeders to move easily among fallen leaves and debris under the cover of the foliage, which is their preferred location. However their distinctive large dark eyes can often reveal their presence. Collectively they are aptly known as a watch of nightingales.

A mythical tale, referred to by various poets, suggests that when the nightingale sings it presses its breast against a thorn. Richard Barnfield (1574-1627) refers to this romantic notion in his 'Poems: In Divers Humours, An Ode'.

> *Everything did banish and moan,*
> *Save the nightingale alone:*
> *She, poor bird, as all forlorn,*
> *Leaned her breast up-till a thorn,*
> *And there sung the dolefull'st ditty,*
> *That to hear it was great pity.*

For a bird renowned for its song there was no escape from the persecution of a caged existence. Although many cages were

elaborate constructions of wood, others were of a simple design made during quieter periods in later life, to be hung either inside or outside the home for the simple pleasure of the inhabitants, who did not regard it as a cruel practice. Edmund Spenser in 'The Shepherd's Calendar' written in 1578-9 recalls:

> *To make fine cages for the Nightingale,*
> *And baskets of bulrushes was my wont.*

Capturing nightingales supposedly ceased with the Wild Bird Protection Acts of 1880. Reading an account by Richard Jefferies (1848-1887) in *Chronicles of the Hedges* one is made fully aware of the unnecessary suffering that it caused:

> *A couple of roughs would come down from town and silence a whole grove. The nightingale would watch the trap being laid, and pounce on the alluring mealworm as soon as the trapper was out of sight. It would be quite as much curiosity as gluttony that led to its fate; and the fate was a sad one. These birds are so shy that it is nearly impossible to keep them alive. They literally beat themselves to death against their prison wires. So for the first fortnight of captivity the wings were tied, and the bird kept caged in the dark. Light was gradually let in – at first a few pinholes in the paper that covered the cage. The captive would peck and peck at these till a rent was made and in time the paper would come away. The mortality was pitiable. Seventy per cent of these little creatures that were singing a week before in full-throated ease in the Surrey lanes would be flung into the gutters of Seven Dials or Whitechapel.*

The poet John Keats (1795-1821) who tragically died at an early age too, wrote movingly of the nightingale:

> *Thou wast not born for death, immortal bird,*
> *No hungry generations tread thee down;*
> *The voice I hear this passing night was heard*
> *In ancient days by emperor and clown.*

OSPREY

On a gaunt and shattered tree
By the black cliffs of obsidian
I saw the nest of the osprey.
Nothing remained of the tree
For this lonely eyrie
Save the undaunted bole.
J B RITTENHOUSE, 'A Bird-Lover's Anthology'

OSPREY *(Pandion haliaetus)*. Written as ospray in 1460, the present spelling dates from 1544. The word was apparently borrowed from the Old French *osfraie*, which came from the Latin ossifraga, literally bone-breaker. There was some earlier confusion with the sea eagle, which may account for two of the common names for the osprey – eagle fisher and fishing eagle. The bird is also known as the white-tailed eagle with which it was often confused, bald buzzard, fish hawk and mullet hawk, the latter from the bird's partiality to the fish which it hunts in estuarine waters. It favours small trout and salmon, for which it was once persecuted, pike, bream, carp, roach and perch.

The dramatic way in which osprey dive towards a loch, hitting the water with their strong white-breeched, outstretched legs is quite spectacular. Strong feet with sharp talons, with spiny scales on the underside and a reversible outer toe, enable the osprey to snatch fish weighing up to three kilograms, from below the surface of the water, which they hold head-first, torpedo-style. Then, with a great surge of energy, wings outstretched, it emerges shaking its plumage violently, and in a cloud of swirling spray lifts its prey to the skies. Unfortunately for the fish this is a memorable sight.

Because they are such successful hunters, our ancestors believed that the birds had a special power to attract fish as they circled and hovered above the water. In 1594 George Peel, in 'The Battle of Alcazar', suggests this possibility:

I will provide thee of a princely osprey,
That, as he flieth over fish in pools,
The fish shall turn their glistering bellies up
And thou shalt take thy liberal choice of all.

And similiarly the following century:

The Osprey oft here seene, though seldome here it breeds,
Which over them the Fish no sooner doe espies,
But (betwixt him and them, by an antipathy)
Turning their bellies up, as though their death they saw,
They at his pleasure lye to stuffe his glutt'nous maw

wrote Michael Drayton in his 'Song' of Lincolnshire (1613) where osprey were said to be often seen. Later this belief was, incorrectly, attributed to an oily substance contained in its body which was said to act as a bait, attracting the fish to the surface of the water. Apart from this supposed fatal attraction, the osprey was thought to have one foot like a hawk to prey with, and one like a goose to swim with.

Ospreys migrate to West Africa where they spend the winter, returning to the conifer trees and island ruins among the lochs in Scotland in about March and April. The eyrie which is used annually, is made of sticks and lined with grasses and tends to be large but inconspicuous. The eggs, two or three in number, are white, blotched with deep chocolate or reddish-brown.

Long-winged with a shortish tail, the osprey is unmistakable from below, its white body and wing linings contrasting with greyish flight feathers and black wrist patches. It has quite a small head, the white feathers highlighted by a brown eye band which blends into the warm brown plumage of the upper parts of the body.

There can be fewer more persecuted birds in history than the osprey, which at one time was a common visitor to the large estuaries round our coasts. Sadly, they had been hunted to extinction by the turn of this century. During the sixteenth century, according to William Harrison writing in 1577, they were to be found in the countryside too, although in this instance it was the young birds that were used as a decoy for obtaining food:

> *osparies, which breed with us in parks and woods, whereby the keepers of the same do reap in breeding time no small commodity; for so soon almost as the young are hatched, they tie them to the butt ends or ground ends of sundry trees, where the old ones finding them, do never cease to bring fish unto them, which the keepers take and eat from them.*

Generally they were shot by gamekeepers in a ruthless bid to protect fish and game birds. However there were others who were prepared take a potshot at anything flying or perched, which unfortunately included some naturalists. From these various factions came those who supplied taxidermists with what was becoming increasingly rare specimens, providing exhibits for natural history museums and trophies for private collectors. As if that was not enough, greedy egg-collectors too furthered the decline until their exploits were banned under the Protection of Birds Act. The lengths people went to find the osprey were quite extraordinary.

According to Robert Dougall in his *A Celebration of Bird*, one notorious professional egg-collector, Lewis Dunbar, who fortunately emigrated to Australia, described a raid he made in 1848 on a traditional nesting site – an eyrie perched on a tower, in a ruined castle on Loch Eilein. The expedition not only involved a twenty mile walk, a swim in the loch, having his bare legs stung by nettles and fortunately great difficulty in trying to find the easiest way to the nest, of which he wrote 'I climbed up and secured three eggs, and put them in my bonnet, placed the latter on my head, and took to the water again. On reaching the shore, a woman at the gamekeeper's house saw me and fled quickly inside.' Which would not be surprising, as he must have been naked. On another occasion when he was in the water he was taken with cramp and hauled out by his cousin and 'after dressing, we forded the river which was very high at the time; and on going across with my cousin on my back, I stumbled . . . this put an end to our adventures'.

Nevertheless the return of the osprey, a very special bird, after half a century to Scotland in 1959, is now bird lore. After what could only be described as an extremely well organized plan, Operation Osprey, carried out by totally dedicated people, came to a heart-warming conclusion in the spring of that year when three young were reared successfully in an eyrie at the top of a tall Scots pine at Loch Garten on Speyside. This singular event helped to publicize the invaluable conservation work carried out by the Royal Society for the Protection of Birds. After a successful appeal the Society was able to purchase the nest site, with fifteen hundred acres of forest, loch and moorland which is now a reserve for all time. The osprey is now thriving. Plans are also underway to introduce osprey chicks to Rutland Water in Lincolnshire, where parent birds have already been stopping off to feed.

BARN OWL

Grave bird, that shelter'd in thy lonely bower,
On some tall oak with ivy overspread,
Or in some silent barn's deserted shed,
Or mid the fragments of some ruin'd tower,
Still, as of old, at this sad solemn hour.
'To the Owl'. THOMAS RUSSELL

BARN OWL (*Tyto alba*) The general term for any species of owl goes back via Middle English 'oule' to Old English 'ule'. A small or nestling owl, known as an owlet, dates back to 1534. Howlet and owlard have similar origins. Familiar names include white owl, yellow owl, silver owl, screech owl, scritch owl, hissing owl, screaming owl, Jenny howlet, Madge howlet, moggy, Madge, hobby owl, gillihowlet, ullat and the Gaelic, *Cailleach-oidhche Gheal* – white old woman of the night.

This bird of the night, although some are partly diurnal, is one of the most widely distributed birds in the world. Unfortunately in Britain their numbers are in decline, partly due to loss of habitat, mainly in old farm buildings where in the past farmers encouraged them to stay in the barns where their corn was stored, as an effective means of vermin control, even making holes for easier access. Changes in agricultural practices, in

the process of which the birds have lost their prey-rich field edges, rough pasture and hedgerow have not been helpful. Nevertheless they are and always have been welcome on farmland. The barn owl is a very distinctive-looking bird with a large, round-topped head and dark eyes set in a white heart-shaped face, with under-parts tapering to long feathered legs and sharp, taloned toes.

Although they often nest in buildings, where they lay four to seven white eggs at intervals, they also favour holes in trees. From these nest sites a strange variety of hisses and snores may be heard. Sometimes a tell-tale pile of large black pellets of undigested prey can indicate occupation or a roost. Many people associate the owl with ruins and old churches or, more precisely, towers, as Alfred, Lord Tennyson in the first verse of the song, 'The Owl', wrote:

> *When cats run home and light is come,*
> *And dew is on the ground,*
> *And the far off stream is dumb,*
> *And the whirring sail goes round,*
> *And the whirring sail goes round;*
> *Alone and warming his five wits,*
> *The white owl in the belfry sits.*

In folklore the owl is a symbol of meditation, night, silence and wisdom. An all-seeing, flesh eater, it typifies a ghost, messenger of witches. The owl's cry in the vicinity of a house foretells calamity, death and sickness – unless you can make the sign of the cross before the call fades away. In Greek mythology it is sacred to Asclepius, deity of healing; Minerva, ancient Italian goddess of the dawn and rustic life, to whom both the owl and the serpent were sacred; and Athena, one of the twelve Olympian deities, goddess of wisdom. Coins were minted showing her head on one side and the owl on the other.

> *Our worth the Grecian sages knew,*
> *They gave our sires the honour due;*
> *They weighed the dignity of fowls,*

And pry'd into the depth of Owls.
Athens the seat of learned fame,
With general voice revered our name;
On merit, the title was conferred,
And all adored th' Athenian Bird

wrote John Gay (1685-1732) in 'Two Owls and the Sparrow'.

Ancient Egyptians feared owls and believed they brought evil and death. Those in authority took advantage of this fear; When a king wished to dismiss a minister an owl was dispatched as a sign that his services were no longer required – the outcome was usually suicide. The Romans believed that if a barn owl perched on the roof of a house it meant that someone inside was going to die – a belief which persisted in parts of Britain until this century. Older writers seemed to have regarded the owl as an abominable and unlucky bird, whose hoarse and dismal voice was an ominous warning of some dire calamity or great misfortune. Geoffrey Chaucer wrote in *The Parliament of Fowls*: 'The oules eke, that of deth the bode bringeth'.

Great significance was attached to the blood-curdling screech of the owl as William Shakespeare noted in *Richard III*: 'The owl shriek'd at thy birth, an evil sign . . .' and in *Macbeth*: 'It was the owl that shriek'd, the fatal bellman Which gives the sternest good night', and as an ominous sign preceeding the death of Julius Caesar:

. . . yesterday the bird of night did sit
Even at noon-day, upon the market place,
Hooting and shrieking.

No self-respecting witches' potion was complete without the addition of some part of the owl. William Shakespeare includes the bird in one of the many remedies brewed in *Macbeth*: 'Adder's tongue and blind-worm's sting, Lizard's leg and howlet's wing.'

To counteract the evil charms of witches, herbalists used the owl in their medicines as a sympathetic magic whereby owl broth was used as a cure for whooping cough, and owl's eggs, charred and powdered to improve eyesight; as an omelette, the eggs were said to be an effective hang-over cure! The Romans favoured roast owl as part of their diet. In 350 BC the philosopher Aristotle, who was a keen observer of nature, wrote of the owl *(Noctua)* 'All other birds flock round the Noctua, or as men say "admire", and flying at it buffet it. Wherefore this being nature, fowlers catch with it many different kinds of little birds'. In more recent times, in England bird catchers used a dead owl as a decoy by placing it among 'limed twigs' in the fork of a tree.

In a collection of anonymous madrigal and lute songs, one lay, dated 1607, reflects the unfortunate reputation of the bird.

> *Come, doleful owl, the messenger of woe,*
> *Melancholy's bird, companion of despair,*
> *Sorrow's best friend, and mirth's professed foe,*
> *The chief discourser that delights sad care.*
> *O come, poor owl, and tell thy woes to me,*
> *Which having heard, I'll do the like for thee.*

However by the turn of the eighteenth century Charles Waterton the Yorkshire naturalist heard children singing a slightly jollier song, 'Traveller's Rest' by Philip Gosse, suggesting the bird had seen better days:

> *Once I was a monarch's daughter*
> *And sat on a lady's knee*
> *But am now a nightly rover,*
> *Banished to the ivy tree,*
> *Crying, Hoo hoo, hoo hoo, hoo hoo.*
> *Hoo! Hoo! Hoo! My feet are cold!*
> *Pity me for here you see me.*
> *Persecuted, poor and old!*

Legend must have the last word on this unusual bird by suggesting that the barn owl was originally a beautiful fair-skinned lady with silvery blond hair. A wizard, thinking she was too vain, changed her into a bird with a screech no one could bear.

PARTRIDGE

The partridge makes no nest but on the ground
Lays many eggs and I have often found
Sixteen or eighteen in a beaten seat
When tracing oer the fields or weeding wheat
They lay in furrows or an old land rig
Brown as the pheasants only not so big.
(MNB9, 96) JOHN CLARE

PARTRIDGE *(Perdix perdix)*. The present spelling of partridge appeared in 1579; however, there are earlier references to partrich and, in 1400, pertriche. A different form was used in the north of England, partrick which became patrick, and in Scotland pertrick then pairtrick to paitrick, respectively. Naturally Robert Burns (1759-1796) favoured paitrick in his 'Elegy on Captain Matthew Henderson':

And mourn, ye whirring paitrick brood;
He's gane for ever

The introduction of a number of species of partridge to Britain, such as the red-legged or French partridge, sometime causes confusion with our handsome native bird which is known as English partridge, grey partridge or common partridge.

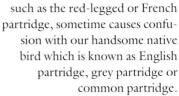

Perdix literally means partridge and in Greek mythology a sun deity. Perdix was the nephew and pupil of the inventor Daedalus, who was so proud of his own achievements that he could not bear a rival. According to legend Perdix was walking along the seashore, when he picked up the spine of a fish. Imitating it, he took a piece of iron and notched it on the edge and made a saw. He also fashioned two pieces of iron into a pair of compasses. Jealous of his nephew's work, Daedalus attempted to push him off a high tower. The goddess Minerva, who favoured ingenuity, saw him falling and changed him into a partridge. Strange as it may seem, the bird does not build in trees, avoids high places and flies low to the ground. In folklore the partridge is a spring migrant sacred to fertility, sun deities and to love goddesses because of its carnal passions. The male supposedly practises sodomy when the female sits on her eggs. According to tradition the hen can be become impregnated by the sound of the cock's voice or his scent in the wind. The dance of the partridge is an orgiastic war dance performed by cocks for hens. They hobble on one foot, keeping the other one in readiness to strike a rival. The male is said to become so absorbed in his dance that if a man comes close and kills one of the dancers, the others continue undeterred.

In more recent times a barbaric custom required a partridge to be lamed and caged. Its love call attracted other cocks, who in turn were caught by hunters. The more rivals the caged cock saw killed, the more gleeful his cry was alleged to sound. *Perdix, toujours perdix*, means too much of the same thing. According to Walpole a French king was reproved by his priest for conjugal infidelity. The king asked him what food he enjoyed the best, the priest replied 'partridge'. So the monarch ordered it to be served every day until the poor man was heartily sick of eating it. Time passed and the king visted his confessor to ask if all was well. He replied, 'Mais oui, perdrix, toujour perdrix.' 'Ah! ah!' replied the amorous king, 'and one mistress is all very well, but not "*perdrix, toujours perdrix*."'

In some parts of Europe the partridge was a weather oracle:

If the partridge sings when the rainbow spans the sky
There is no better sign of wet than when it isn't dry.

For centuries the birds have been bred and hunted with dogs not only as a country pastime but as a welcome addition, in their season, for the pot. John Gay (1685-1732) in 'Rural Sports', not only uses the collective noun for a family of partridge, a covey, but includes a seasonal feeding ground after the harvest has been gathered in:

See how the well-taught pointer leads the way:
The scent grows warm, he stops, he springs the prey;
The flutt'ring covey from the stubble rise,
And on swift wing divide the sounding skies;
The scatt'ring lead pursues the certain sight,
And death in thunder overtakes their flight.

In the autumn they flock together in large parties in open fields, the scene resembling a busy market with the customers displaying their wares, fighting and generally showing off. A blur of orange faces, speckled vests, barred flanks and distinctive horse-shoe marks on the belly (particularly the male) eventually concludes with a pairing off by the spring. For their nesting sites they favour the dense undergrowth of plants and grasses bordering open fields, sheltered by hedges. The nest is often little more than a hollow in the ground lined with leaves and grass in which a single large clutch of unmarked olive-brown eggs are laid from the end of April onwards. The chicks delight the eye – darting fluffy balls on pin-stick legs – busily facing the problems of survival as soon as they hatch.

The Romans practised intensive rearing of birds in special enclosures and may have kept partridges in captivity here.

Stewed partridge was a popular medieval dish which consisted of beef or mutton broth, red wine, marrow, cloves, mace, and whole peppers: 'when thou shalt serve him forth cast into the pot powdered ginger, salt and saffron'.

The Compleat Housewife, a Georgian book, advises when choosing a partridge that 'if they have fed lately on green

wheat, and their crops be full, smell to their mouths, lest crops be tainted'. *Warne's Model Cookery*, second edition, published in 1893, recommended that partridges be 'hung' for a few days before being plucked, drawn and wiped inside and out. If the head is left on, it should be brought round and fixed on to the point of a skewer. When trussed the bird is roasted before an open fire, basted frequently and frothed with flour and butter before serving with gravy and bread sauce. Partridge soup, consisting of a shank of beef, four slices of ham or bacon, ten peppercorns, one stick of celery, two onions, three ounces of butter, two pounds of gravy beef, a glass of white wine, a pinch of cayenne pepper and two old partridges provided ample sustenance for a winter's day.

St Partridge's Day is 1 September, the first day of the season for shooting the bird. For those who have neither seen nor eaten the bird the name must be familiar from a verse in 'The Twelve Days of Christmas' in the jolly Christmas song, with its Partridge in a Pear Tree, the source of which must remain a mystery.

PEREGRINE FALCON

PEREGRINE FALCON *(Falco peregrinus)*. The Latin name *Falco peregrinus* was given by an early naturalist, Albertus Magnus of Cologne (1206-1280) in 1250, a term he applied to a young peregrine which had been trapped when making its first long distance flight from unknown parts and adapted from Old French *faucon pelerin*. The peregrine falcon is also known as blue hawk, blue-backed falcon, spotted falcon, hunting hawk, stock hawk, duck hawk, game hawk and goshawk.

Until recent times, particularly during this century, it was a much persecuted bird, mainly by gamekeepers, sportsmen, farmers and collectors who overestimated the damage done by these magnificent birds. In retrospect it is hard to believe that they were shot during the World War II to protect pigeons carrying secret messages. By the 1960s pesticides had also taken their toll with the discovery of thin-shelled eggs, which were easily broken, caused through the peregrine eating prey that had been contaminated by insects. Nevertheless, in spite of these setbacks, during the breeding season they can now be seen flying over mountains, moorlands and sea-cliffs. They nest – a bare scrape – on ledges and crevices occasionally using an abandoned raven's nest, where they lay three or four lightly dappled tawny to reddish-brown eggs. The larger female peregrine with whitish grey head, back and wings, white to warm buff under-parts with beautiful patterned black bars and lightly barred underwings, performs spectacular aerial displays with her similarly feathered mate. Their very presence, for instance on an estuary, will cause immediate panic amongst the bird population. The speed of their stoop – by which their victim is caught – can reach up to 200 miles per hour and is said to be a memorable climactic moment - for the onlooker!

Peregrines were the falcons of kings and nobles when hawking, which has a long and honourable history, was a popular pastime in every European court. The development of effective guns in the seventeenth century started the decline in the sport from which it is presently enjoying a renaissance. The art of falconry would seem to have its roots in Arabia centuries ago, reaching England around AD 860, and is thought to have been introduced by French nobles. By the Middle Ages they were protected by royal decree. The death penalty was the punishment for anyone who took a wild falcon or interfered with its nest, and it was at this time values were established for the various birds. A gyrfalcon was assigned to the king, falcon or tercel gentle a prince, falcon of the rock a duke, falcon peregrine an earl, bastard hawk for a baron, sacre and sacret for a knight, lanare and lanret for a squire, merlin for a lady, hoby a young man, goshawk for a yeoman, tercel for a poor man, sparrowhawk for a priest, musket for a holy-water clerk and kestrel for a knave. In falconry the male peregrine is called tiercel (tassel or tercel) gentle, because it is about a third, that is a tierce, of the size of the female falcon.

> *The lanner and the lanneret*
> *Thy colours bear as banneret;*
> *The goshawk and her tercel, roused,*
> *With tears attend thee as new bowsed.*

wrote Richard Lovelace on the death of a favourite falcon in aerial combat with its prey, a heron. Different parts of the hawk's (which is a generic term) body have a special name, likewise the dress of a hawk, including hood – a cover for the head to keep the hawk in the dark, and jesses – the little straps by which the leash is fastened to the legs.

> *And now at length let pity move*
> *To stoop unto his lure.*
> *A hood of silk and silver bells,*
> *New gifts I promise thee:*

wrote an anonymous sixteenth-century poet of his falcon. There are also special terms used in falconry, which is the breeding and training of hawks to take a wild quarry for sport. A falconer is a person who also hunts with hawks. Such training is briefly described in an extract from the anonymous ninth century poem 'The Fortunes of Men':

> *He puts on straps,*
> *And feeds the fettered, wing-bold bird,*
> *Tempting the sky-speeder with bits of food*
> *Until the falcon, growing gentle*
> *In all his deeds, obeys the food-giver,*
> *Taught to sit on his trainer's hand.*

In the early stages of training man and bird spend as much time as possible together; some would be inseparable for a whole week to establish a bond. Then the bird was thrown at a lure of feathers and meat swung on a rope. When it captured the lure it was rewarded with food and rested quietly, generally hooded, on its master's wrist between flights, eventually retrieving wild birds for its master. Peregrines were used to hunt wildfowl to feed the large households of the upper classes, who would also employ a bird-catcher for the smaller birds. Kings Ethelbert and Canute, Alfred the Great and Mary Queen of Scots were all said to have been enthusiasts of the sport.

In folklore the falcon is a symbol of fire, immortality, modesty, storms, sun and wind. It is a bird of omen, a fierce hunter which always returns to the one who releases it. In Christianity a trained falcon typifies the convert or holy man; a wild falcon typifies the evil man, and the plumage of the bird symbolizes high, swift flight. In mythology the falcon was a symbol of Horus, a solar god constantly identified with Apollo and represented by a falcon or a falcon-headed god. Under the name of Hor, which in Eygptian sounds like a word meaning sky, the Egyptians referred to the falcon which they saw soaring high above their heads, and many thought of the sky as a divine falcon, whose eyes were the sun and the moon. The worshippers of the bird were numerous and powerful, for it was carried as a totem on pre-historic standards from earliest times. The birds merited mummification and were interred in pottery sarcophagi. The hieroglyph which represents the idea of 'god' was a falcon on a perch. In Norse mythology the falcon is an attribute of Freyja, wife of Odin, who was alleged to hover above the earth in her feather dress (clouds).

PHEASANT

Ah! what avail his glossy, varying dyes,
His purple crest, and scarlet-circled eyes,
The vivid green his shining plumes unfold,
His painted wings, and breast that flames with gold?
'Windsor Forest,' ALEXANDER POPE

PHEASANT *(Phasianus colchicus)*. The word pheasant and the scientific name *Phasianus* and various other European names all come from the same Greek source, *Phasis*, a river south of the Caucasus on the Black Sea where pheasants were to be found. Common names for the bird include black pheasant, ffeasant, ffesont, comet and cock-up (male).

The pheasant was almost certainly introduced to Britain by the Romans, who kept them in large aviaries for domestic use in their native land. In earlier times it is very unlikely that many of our so called British pheasant would have survived in the wild. Nevertheless there were certainly wild pheasants after the Norman Conquest. During the reign of Henry VIII, and possibly other monarchs too, the penalty for stealing a pheasant's egg was a year in prison, indicating a royal prerogative. It was not until the late eighteenth century that a white-collared species was introduced – the Chinese ringed-necked pheasant. This closely related sub-species quickly interbred with the

local population and now a cock pheasant without the distinctive smart neckband is a rare sighting.

The understated elegance of the milk-chocolate brown markings on buff plumage of the female bird is a sharp contrast to the colourful display of the male. And if that should prove not enough to attract a partner, particularly during the mating season – many partners in fact – he performs scuttling movements, twisting over his long tail, trailing the near wing and inflating his facial wattles. Once the females are safely on the nest, camouflaged under the protection of a bramble or in thick grass where a hollow is made – a nest which is rather sketchily lined with a few blades of grass and dead leaves – he almost ignores them.

The cock announces his ownership with a distinctive harsh crow and shorter *hic-u*. One clutch of eggs is laid each year towards the end of April or during May. The number of eggs varies, averaging ten or twelve, broadly rounded and olive-brown in colour. In earlier times hawks were used to hunt pheasants, as the anonymous fifteenth-century poet reveals:

I took my hawk, me for to play,
My spaniel runnung by my side
A pheasant hen then gan I see;
My hounde put her soon to flight;
I let my hawk unto her flee
To me it was a dainty sight.

In 'Noah's Flood', Michael Drayton makes an unlikely pairing:

The goshawk and the pheasant there do twin
And in the Ark are percht upon one pin.

Trapping birds exercised the mind of our ancestors and many ingenious devices were conjured up, usually by poachers. The noose or snare was used for catching ground-running birds, and was concealed in hedgerows or under fences where the birds usually passed. Various designs developed from this. One in particular, known as 'the hangman's trap,' required a bent sapling serving as a spring, to hang over a hole with various strings, a noose and a twig, which resulted in the bird being 'swung aloft as on a gibbet'.

Victorian poachers with access to champagne, well, the empty bottle, rammed it neck-down into soft snow sufficiently firmly to leave an impression of the bottle after it had been removed. The hole left by the neck was filled with soaked dried peas. A pheasant will lean over and manage to reach the peas on top, but there will come a stage when it topples over and gets its head stuck fast in the hole. A similar method was to use a jam-jar buried up to its neck in a furrow. The most gentle method, however, when pheasants were fairly common in England, was practised during the summer. When the cock invaded a cottage garden to steal peas, the trap was a paperbag and raisins! The trick was quite simple: one smeared the inside of the bag with treacle or gum, put a few raisins in the bottom and propped the bag up amongst the peas. When the pheasant poked his head in the bag he could not see where to go and stood still until rescued. Before the last war, on most sporting estates hen pheasants were not shot after Boxing Day, whereas now it is not uncommon for them to be shot until February. Officially the shooting season only lasts from 1 October to 31 January. A graphic description of the seasonal slaughter is given by Pope in his poem 'Windsor Forest':

> *See, from the brake the whirring pheasant springs,*
> *And mounts exulting on triumphant wings:*
> *Short is his joy; he feels the fiery wound,*
> *Flutters in blood, and panting beats the ground*

According to the children's calendar rhyme the season starts when:

> *Brown October brings the pheasant,*
> *Then to gather nuts is pleasant*

It was not only the taste of the bird but also the beautiful plumage of the cock pheasant that made it a handsome addition to a medieval banquet. Once cooked the feathers would be returned to the roasted bird and presented to the guests at the table as nature originally intended. A medieval recipe for pheasant, which should be well hung (otherwise it was said to taste like brown chicken) was as follows: pluck the bird carefully as the skin will be soft, and flour with oatmeal. Brush inside and outside of the carcass with melted butter and insert a piece of well-pounded steak. Serve with bread sauce, fried crumbs and red gooseberry jelly. An alternative stuffing was apple and raisin or a small bunch of red currants. When pheasants were the preserve of the gentry, poachers thought it prudent to disregard the culinary advice of 'hanging' the bird for a few days by swiftly consuming the evidence.

In folklore the pheasant symbolizes beauty, luxury, gourmandizing and mother love. The dream significance is a happy event. In Greek mythology. Jason and his Argonauts brought the birds back from Georgia after his search for the Golden Fleece. The pretty white flower, pheasant's eye *(Narcissus poeticus)* is a charming floral tribute to a bird with such a distinctive feature. In the language of flowers it signifies 'I cannot forget you'.

QUAIL

I love to muse oer meadows newly mown
Where withering grass perfumes the sultry air
Where bees search round with sad and weary drone
In vain for flowers that bloomed but newly there
While in the juicy corn the hidden quail
Cries 'wet my foot' and hid as thoughts unborn.
'Summer Moods', JOHN CLARE

QUAIL *(Coturnix coturnix)*. Quail was introduced by the Normans and entered the English language in the fourteenth century as 'quayle', the present spelling dating from 1684. Many of the country names are imitative of the quail's voice, which consists of three sharp notes such as wet-my-feet, quick-me-dick, but-for-but and wet-my-lip. Nevertheless James Riley, in his poem 'Days Gone By', likened the sound to that of a song bird!

The apples in the orchard, and the pathway through the rye;
The chirrup of the robin, and the whistle of the quail
As he piped across the meadows sweet as any nightingale.

John Clare, on the other hand, had a different interpretation when he wrote of it: 'tho it is seen more often and is easily urged to take wing it makes an odd noise in the grass as if it said "wet my foot wet my foot" which Weeders and Haymakers hearken to as a prophecy of rain and believe in it as an infallable sign.' Other strange names include quailzie, deadchick, corncrake, rine and throsher. The quail is a rare breeding bird which is also Britain's only migrant game bird. It is found mainly in the southern counties of England on arable land, limestone or chalk or open downs. Its nest is merely a scrape lined with a few bits of grass or local vegetation, often corn, clover or bean crops. Quails usually lay seven to twelve buff-coloured eggs marbled with brown, which the female incubates for about three weeks. Quail are the smallest European game bird and are similiar in shape and colour to the partridge, sandy-brown above and paler below with light streaks on the flanks. The female is less colourful, and the cock has a stripe over the eye.

The call of the bird is said to have a ventriloquist's effect, and sportsmen say it can throw its voice. The sound of the bird, either 'wet my foot' or as others would have it 'wet my lips' is more like 'whit whit whit', and is easier to hear in the quiet of the evening although it can be distinguished during the day. The call of the hen can have a bizarre effect on the cock. He runs up and circles round her, puffing up his neck and breast feathers, stretching his neck and dragging his wings along the ground. There are 'duets' between male and female, and the male does stay nearby during incubation.

In folklore the quail is a symbol of resurrection as well as lasciviousness. In mythology it is sacred to Apollo and Melkarth, the Phoenician sun deity, who was a god of the underworld until the days lengthened at the winter solstice. Sacred to him were the oak and quail. When the quail arrives in March, the oak is said to begin to come into leaf to celebrate its resurrection.

In weather lore when quails are heard in the evening expect fair weather next day.

An ancient party trick which defies belief required the dissolved eyes of a quail, or a sea tench, and a little water, to be placed in a glass vessel for seven days, then added to a little oil. If you put some of this in the candle and light it among the company, they would look on themselves like devils on fire, so that everyone would run away!

This smallest of European game birds is mentioned in the Bible in Exodus, where migratory flocks twice saved the Israelites from starvation: 'and it came to pass that at even the quails, came up and covered the camp'; the 'at even' according to J H Gurney (Early Annals of Ornithology) is significant because quails like many migrants, fly at night. The ancient Greek heirs to the Aegean empire hunted game which was plentiful in the countryside, which of course included the quail, and so it is hardly surprising they were targets for the falconers in medieval times when the enemy, according to Chaucer was:

the hardy sparhawk eke,
The quaile's foe

In a recipe from the middle of the last century one was advised that the quail must be plucked, singed, and drawn. You should then cut off its wings at the first pinion, leaving the feet, and pass a skewer through the pinions and wings. Next cover the breasts with vine leaves and a slice of fat bacon, secured with a skewer, which can be tied to a spit. Roast them for ten or twelve minutes before a brisk fire, serve hot with a good gravy. Traditionally, quail was wrapped in vine leaves and roasted like any other small bird; the vine leaves were left on but the birds were placed on a fresh leaf when served.

Unfortunately quails' eggs have always been a popular delicacy, but nowadays they do not have the same value attached to them because they are readily available. Traditionally they were served, hard-boiled and piled into a basket, where guests were able to help themselves by peeling their own eggs, which is rather a fiddly task, and seasoning them with salt.

RAVEN

Upon the collar of an huge old oak
Year after year boys mark a curious nest
Of twigs made up a faggot near in size
And boys to reach it try all sorts of schemes
But not a twig to reach with hand or foot
Sprouts from the pillared trunk
'The Raven's Nest', JOHN CLARE

RAVEN *(Corvus corax)*. Raven is a very old name going back to Old English 'hraefn'. The Norse god Odin was also Hrafnagud, the Raven God. He allegedly carried a raven on either shoulder who flew round the world, reporting back to him on everything that was happening. A Norse standard, the Landeyda, which depicted a raven was said to have magical powers. When they marched to victory the raven flew erect, but when defeat was imminent the raven drooped its wings.

Other familiar names for the raven are corbie, which was sometimes applied to the crow, croupy craw, fiach and ralph or rolfe.

The raven, called Rolfe,
His plain-song to sol-fa;

wrote John Skelton (1460-1529) in an extract from 'Philip Sparrow'. The large size of the raven distinguishes it from other members of the crow family. Most ravens are crag dwellers, where they often build, although they also nest in groups in the canopy of trees. Their large nests, often repaired from previous years, are constructed from small branches and twigs and lined in layers of earth, then with roots and plant material and finally wool, hair and fine grasses. Between three and six greenish-blue eggs with dark brown markings are laid in March. Ravens occupy their territories all year round and can be seen performing spectacular acrobatic displays, diving and tumbling at a great height, carrying pebbles and sticks which they drop and then swoop down to recover with their beak or claw. Their repertoire also includes gliding and soaring off the thermals with an occasional upside-down, belly-uppermost, short-burst glide thrown in for good measure'.

Ravens can be seen on valley sides, mountains, sea cliffs, woods and moorland. The entirely black plumage of this powerful bird has a blue, purplish and greenish gloss which glistens in the sunlight as the raven occasionally hops, but more often walks with a distinctive stately gait, reminiscent of an archdeacon. Long pointed throat feathers drop like a beard below the powerful bill, giving a slightly sinister look to the head. They eat small mammals, frogs, lizards, insects and refuse, although dead sheep are their main food source. In earlier times, however, gallows provided aerial food stations, as the anonymous ninth century verse, 'The Fortunes of Men', reveals:

> *The dark coated raven rips out his eyes,*
> *Tears at the flesh of the lifeless corpse,*
> *But his hands cannot beat off the hateful bird,*
> *The black winged ghoul, for his life is gone.*

In folklore the raven signifies intelligence, cruelty, death, the devil, disease, falseness, foreknowledge, foulness, greed, ill-omen, impudence, rapaciousness, war, wickedness, to plunder or prey – also as well as the soul of a wicked person. The raven is sacred to Asclepius, deity of healing in Greek mythology; Apollo son of Zeus and Leto, the great patron of augurs (people who pretended to tell future events by the singing, flight and feeding of birds) who were called companions and attendants of that deity. The raven is also associated with Cronus, deity of time in the sense of eternal duration; Elijah, whom the bird was appointed to feed, by Heaven, when he fled from the rage of Ahab, although it is said 'He that employed a raven to be a feeder of Elias may employ the same bird as a messenger of death to others'. The bird is also sacred to Saturn, the ancient

Roman deity of harvest, seed sower and answerer, who in later legend devoured his children. And to Noah, who was directed by God to build an ark of gopher wood, as a shelter for his family, and a pair of every living thing. An eighth-century verse describes an event in the aftermath of the flood:

The son of Lamech let a black raven
Fly out of the Ark on the empty flood.
Noah believed that if in his flight
He did not find land, the bird would be forced
To search the wide expanse of the sea
For the ship. But his hopes were all deceived:
The fiend soon fell upon floating corpses;
The dark feathered bird did not come back.

However, in an earlier legend, the raven had white plumage which changed to black when it began the grisly feast. Despite this association, in Christian art the raven is assigned to saints Anthony, Apollonaris, Benedict and Vincent because the bird guarded or provided them with food when they lived as hermits.

The superstitious generally regarded the sight or sound of a raven with fear and trepidation:

> *The boding raven on her cottage sate*
> *And with hoarse croaking warn'd us of our fate.*

Wrote John Gay in his 'Dirge', whereupon it was necessary to make a will. Samuel Butler made a similar assumption:

> *Is it not ominous in all countries*
> *When crows and ravens croak upon trees?*

The number of ravens seen at one time was also significant, as the anonymous old rhyme, 'The Unlucky Sailor', suggests:

> *Three ravens sit in yonder glade,*
> *And evil will hap, I'm sore afraid,*
> *Ere we reach our journey's end.*
> *And what have the ravens with us to do?*
> *Does their sight betoken us evil?*
> *To see one raven is lucky 'tis true,*
> *But it's certain misfortune to light upon two,*
> *And meeting with three is the devil.*

For the less fearful the raven was useful in weather lore. Two such forecasts are given in the *Prognostication Everlasting* of Leonard Digges (1556):

> *When the Crowe or the Raven gapeth against the Sunne,*
> *in Summer, heate foloweth*

And:

> *If they busy themselves in proyning or washyng, and that in*
> *Winter, loke for Raine.*

And in a translation of Virgil's *Georgics* by Dryden:

> *Then thrice the ravens rend the liquid air,*
> *And croaking notes proclaim the settled fair.*
> *Then round their airy palaces they fly*
> *To greet the sun; and seized with secret joy,*

When storms are overblown, with food repair
To their forsaken nests and callow care.

A sign of fine weather, according to J Lamb in *Aratus*, is:

When the hoarse raven seeks the shallow waves –
Dips her black head - her wings and body laves.
And e'en the raven from her varying throat
Utters at eve a soft and joyous note.

However Bacon suggests that: 'Ravens, when they croak three or four times and flap their wings fine weather is expected'.

The corbie said unto the craw,
'Johnnie, fling your plaid awa';
The craw says unto the corbie,
'Johnnie, fling your plaid about ye'

In Scotland it is believed that if the raven cries first in the morning, it will be a good day; if the rook, the reverse. When the raven croaks continuously it denotes a strong wind; but if the croaking is interrupted or stifled, or comes at longer intervals, it is a sign of rain.

Thomas Cowper in 'The Raven', wryly describes how this supposedly smart bird fails to notice danger around its own nest.

For ravens, though, as birds of omen,
They teach both conjurors and old women
To tell us what is it befall,
Can't prophesy themselves at all.

The poem concludes with the moral:

Fate steals along with silent tread
Found oftenest in what least we dread.

Numerous stories about the Raven can be found in many parts of the world, particularly in Britain and Europe. They are generally sinister and often terrifying in content. In Christopher Marlowe's *The Jew of Malta* (1633) the bird brings both gloom and doom:

> *The sad presaging raven, that tolls*
> *The sick man's passport in her hollow beak*
> *And in the shadow of the silent night*
> *Doth shake contagion from her sable wing.*

Edgar Allan Poe frightened readers with his book, *The Raven*, and there were even those who believed that the souls of the unbaptized go into ravens and that blind people would be able to see again if they showed kindness to the bird; an ironic suggestion bearing in mind ravens are alleged to take out the eyes of the dead! Nevertheless a bride may have taken some comfort on hearing a raven croaking as she walked to church on her wedding day. This would be a sign of a large family – unfortunately reared in poverty.

It has been suggested that if the ravens leave the Tower of London the Crown will fall. An alternative source advises that if the ravens are lost Britain will be invaded. This belief in the bird as a protector goes back to the thirteenth century when the head of a raven was allegedly buried on Tower Hill to guard the people against their enemies.

R OBIN

The redbreast, sacred to the household gods,
Wisely regardful of the embroiling sky,
In joyless fields and thorny thickets leaves
His shivering mates, and pays to trusted man
His annual visit. Half afraid, he first
Against the window beats; then brisk alights
On the warm hearth.
The Seasons; 'Winter', JAMES THOMSON

ROBIN *(Erithacus rubecula)*. Robin was originally a Christian name, a pet form of Robert, both coming from France with the Normans. The Anglo-Saxons named it *Rudduc*, from the colour of its breast. It was not until 1549 that robin was recorded as a bird name, gradually replacing over the centuries both redbreast and ruddock. Although variations appeared in regional names such as robinet, robin redbreast, robin red-dock, robin ruck and robin rud-dock. Bob robin, Thomas gierdet, ploughman's bird and Tommy-liden were also in popular use. An old riddle teased one to discover

its name:

I'm called by the name of a man,
Yet I am as little as a mouse;
When winter comes I love to be
With my red target near the house.

Britain's robin is a resident bird although their numbers are increased in the winter by less colourful Northern European visitors. Our birds with their upright stance, hop along the ground and, when alarmed, bob and raise their tails. They are bold and friendly and highly territorial, fiercely defending their space from September to May. With their orange-red vest indignantly ruffled they do not hesitate to chase off larger birds and, if necessary, kill other robins. They often nest in unusual places, but are more readily located in a well concealed hole in a bank, on a ledge or garden nestbox. The domed nest of leaves and moss, lined with hair, hides five to seven white eggs with red spots. Although robins sing throughout the year, in early spring the male warbles loudly to proclaim his territory and attract a partner. Courtship starts with song duels at dawn.

In folklore generally, robin redbreast signifies confiding trust and triumph, a New Year spirit who sets out with his birch rod to kill his predecessor, who hides in a bush (see Wren). Legends vary as to how the bird received a red breast; one suggests that the bird murdered its father and that the blood stained the feathers, another that it was singed, while taking water to sinners in hell.

He brings cool dew in his little bill,
And lets it fall on the souls of sin;
You can see the mark on his red breast still
Of fires that scorch as he drops it in

wrote John Greenleaf Whittier, in 'The Robin'. However in the Christian tradition it is said that when our Lord was on his way to Calvary, burdened by the Cross, a robin picked a thorn from His crown, and that the blood which spurted from the wound fell on the bird, dyeing its breast red. In another legend the robin replaces the wren as the firebringer, taking over for the last part of the journey and burning its breast.

> *Kill a robin or a wren*
> *Never prosper, boy or man.*

So warns an old rhyme. It is unlucky to kill or cage a robin or a wren or take their eggs, as an old folk tradition held that the birds were 'God's cock and hen', suggesting they were man and wife.

There are several rhymes associating the robin with the wren and other birds too such as:

> *The robin with the red breast,*
> *The robin and the wren;*
>
> *If ye take them from their nest*
> *Ye'll never thrive again.*

and:

> *The robin with the red breast*
> *The martin and the swallow;*
> *If ye touch one of their eggs*
> *Bad luck will surely follow.*

Harming the bird in any way was said to bring sickness and broken limbs to the perpetrators and their animals too. The ballad 'Who Killed Cock Robin?' published in 1744, is perhaps the best known bird rhyme. Its origins are obscure, but it does include all the familiar birds such as magpie, eagle, owl, lark, rook, kite, swan, wren, bullfinch, martin and, rather oddly, a fish. Concludes with the following verse and names the chief suspect:

> *To all it concerns*
> *This notice apprises*
> *The Sparrow's for trial*
> *At next bird assizes.*

A robin singing on the window sill foretells happiness in love, and if a girl sees a robin before any other bird on St Valentine's Day she will marry a sailor. To have a robin nest near the house is a sign of good luck for the occupants. However if one flies into the house or comes through the back door it is a sign of a death for one of the inhabitantss or someone closely connected to the family.

There are legends associating the robin with charity and the dead, whereby it covers unburied corpses with moss and leaves. Such compassion is mentioned by Michael Drayton in 'The Owl':

> *Covering with moss the dead's unclosed eye,*
> *The little redbreast teacheth charity.*

In *Percy's Reliques* (1765) reference is made to the fairy story 'The Babes in the Wood' where the children, who have died of cold, are tended by the bird:

> *No Burial this pretty pair*
> *Of any man receives*
> *Till Robin Redbreast painfully*
> *Did cover them with leaves.*

A children's rhyme specifies a woodland plant, wild strawberry:

> *And when they were dead*
> *The robin so red*
> *Brought strawberry leaves,*
> *And over them spread.*

Robert Herrick, the Devonshire parson, poet, asked the bird a favour, in his poem 'To Robin Redbreast':

> *Laid out for dead, let thy kindness be*
> *With leaves and moss-work for to cover me:*
> *And while the wood-nymphs my cold corpse inter,*
> *Sing thou my dirge, sweet-warbling chorister!*
> *For epitaph, in foliage, next write this:*
> *Here, here the tomb of Robert Herrick is.*

In weather lore a robin singing in the morning indicates the approach of spring.

Flame-throated robin on the topmost bough
Of the leafless oak, what singest thou?
Hark! he telleth how –
'Spring is coming now; Spring is coming now'

wrote Robert Bridges in 'A Robin'. If the singing is long and loud it is a sign of rain. Should they perch on the topmost branches and whistle it is a sign of a storm approaching. Another sign of bad weather according to J Lamb in 'Aratus' is:

When sparrows ceaseless chirp a dawn of day,
And in their holes the wren and robin stay.

If a robin sings near the ground the weather will be wet, but if one sings on a higher branch it is a sign of fine weather. In *Anecdotes of the Animal Kingdom*, published in 1837, it is forecast that 'On a summer evening, though the weather may be in an unsettled and rainy state, the robin takes his stand on the topmost branch, or on a housetop, singing cheerfully and sweetly. When this is observed, it is an unerring promise of succeeding fine days. Sometimes, though the atmosphere is dry and warm, he may be seen melancholy, chirping and brooding in a bush, or low in the hedge; this promises the reverse of his merry lay and exalted station.'

If the robin sings in the bush
The the weather will be coarse
But if the robin sings on the barn
Then the weather will be warm.

A robin searching for food near a house is a sign of a snow storm. Just as the following verse is a warning to the bird whose life will become very difficult when there is deep snow:

The north wind doth blow,
And we shall have snow
And what will poor robin do then,

Poor thing.
He'll sit in barn and keep himself warm,
And hide his head under his wing,
Poor thing.

Although robins are not mentioned in the Bible or seen in the Holy Land, they are associated with Christmas. When the early festive cards were designed, postmen had a bright red coat so the standard nickname became redbreast or robin. Both names are mentioned in *Framley Parsonage* by Anthony Trollope, published in 1861. Trollope was working in the Post Office as a travelling inspector and is credited with the invention of the pillar-box, which is also bright red. Everyone with a garden seems to have their own robin. Despite the fact that they are here all year long, somehow their reappearance later in the year gives everyone a feeling of pleasure at its return.

Gentleman robin brown as snuff
With spindle legs and bright round eye
Shall be your autumn company.

wrote Vita Sackville-West in 'The Land.' Robins often remain with their human friends for life, even taking food from their hand, particularly meal worms.

S KYLARK

Hail to thee, blithe spirit!
Bird thou never wert,
That from heaven or near it
Pourest thy full heart
In profuse strains of unpremeditated art.
'To a Skylark', PERCY BYSSHE SHELLEY

SKYLARK. *(Alauda arvensis)*. Lark literally means little song and refers to the skylark and the woodlark. Laverock was an earlier name from Old English 'laferce'. Other names include variations of laverock, also rising lark, field lark, short-heeled lark, sky flapper and lintwhite. Skylarks nest on the ground in grass tussocks in open fields, marsh and moorlands, lining their nests with fine grass or hair, in which they lay three to five white eggs with heavy brown markings. The aerial performances and all year round song of the skylark, often flying too high to be seen but not to be heard, have not only endeared and entertained country dwellers but have been a source of inspiration for poets and writers for centuries. A group of skylarks is known as an exaltation, which could not be bettered as a description for these delightful birds.

A simple inscription discovered on a Suffolk drinking cup indicates a contented rural association.

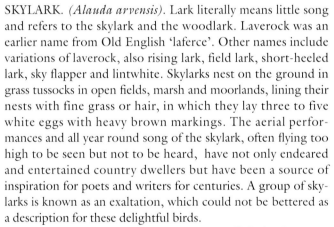

I have lawns, I have bowers, I have fruit
I have flowers
The lark is my morning alarmer
So jolly boys, now here's good speed to the plough
Long life and success to the farmers.

Delightful as the rhyme is, reality appears in the guise of Andrew Boorde in *Dietary of Health* (1547) who assured his readers that 'All manner of small birds be good and light of digestion, except the sparrow, be hard of digestion . . . of all the birds lark is best, then is praised the blackbird and the thrush.'

Leverets and larks, what find we here?
Let us be merry and enjoy such cheer.

Roast larks on breadcrumbs was a very popular dish with our ancestors. According to an ancient recipe, having first caught two dozen birds, 'after picking and cleaning cut off the head and legs, pick out the gizzard, and put seasoning inside them of pepper, salt, nutmeg, and a very little chopped parsley; brush with egg yolks, dip them in bread-crumbs, covering them very thickly, run a small spit through them, and fasten it on a larger one, and put them to roast before a bright fire, basting them constantly with butter, or they will burn. When done arrange them in a circle round a dish, and fill the centre with a pile of crumbs of bread, fried crisp and brown in a little melted butter. Serve with melted butter, with the juice of half a lemon squeezed into it.'

An alternative recipe was the Dunstable Way, whereby the breadcrumbs were piled higher than the larks and cayenne pepper was added. The recipe for Larks à la Macedoine, on the other hand, required eighteen larks, a slice of bacon, sweet herbs, salt, pepper and nutmeg, one pint of gravy, six or eight potatoes, three carrots and three turnips. It instructed: 'Pick and clean the larks, bone them, and stuff them with the livers, a little minced bacon, a few sweet herbs, and a seasoning of salt, pepper and nutmeg, put them into a dish, pour in a little gravy, and bake them in a moderate oven for fifteen minutes.' The cooked potatoes were arranged in a deep border round the edge of a dish, the centre with rings of cooked carrots and turnips and the larks piled round the potatoes, raised high in the centre, with a garnish of vegetables placed in mounds between the birds and served with a little gravy. Plain broiled larks were said to be delicious, although additional breadcrumbs did improve the flavour. Breast of lark was used in pies. The French song 'Alouette, gentille Alouette', which has charmed many English children, actually describes how the bird is plucked.

During the last century there were thousands of larks in the fields; children who could not shoot were sent out amongst the crops with clappers to 'tent larks' (frighten them away). Not only was the skylark eaten but the joy of its song also meant a prison existence for others as Gerald Manley Hopkins wrote in 'The Caged Skylark':

> *As a dare-gale skylark scanted in a dull cage*
> *Man's mounting spirit in his bone-house, mean house, dwells –*
> *That bird beyond the remembering his free fells;*
> *This in drudgery, day-labouring-out life's age.*

Anonymous oral traditions have survived because they were shaped by many people over the centuries. Their meaning is often obscure but possibly the first sighting of a bird or a child's game would revive and repolish half forgotten lines. The following verses refer to the skylark, which has a long straight hind claw.

> *Up in the lift (air) go we*
> *Te-hee, te-hee, te-hee, te-hee!*
> *There's not a shoemaker on the earth*
> *Can make a shoe to me, to me!*
> *Why so, why so, why so?*
> *Because my heel is as long as my toe!*

The following Scottish rhyme refers to getting out of bed in the morning.

Larikie, larikie, lee!.
Wha'll gang up to heaven wi' me?
No the lout that lies in his bed,
No the doolfu' that dreeps his head.

The lark is a symbol of cheerfulness, recklessness and song. In the Christian tradition it typifies humility in priesthood. Many people attatched a great significance to dreams that had an association with birds. To dream of a lark flying suggested coming wealth, singing, pleasant news but to dream of one being caught indicated a loss of money.

Larks were also watched by weather-lorists. If larks fly high and sing long, expect fine weather, but if they congregate in flocks expect severe cold and frost. In Scotland it is said 'As long as the bird sings before Candlemas (2 February) it will be greet after it'.

S NIPE

. . . the ripples of the river lipped the moss along the brink
Where the placid-eyed and lazy footed cattle came to drink,
And the tilting snipe stood fearless of the truant's wayward
*   cry,*
And the splashing of a swimmer, in the days gone by
'The Days Gone By', JAMES W RILEY

SNIPE *(Gallingo gallinago)*. The name occurs in Old English as 'snite' although by 1325 the familiar snipe which basically denotes the bird's characteristic bill, was in common usage too. Local names include such gems as horse gowk, heather bleat, bog bleater, blutter, blitter, ern beater and snippack. Snipe like muddy water-margins with their floral canopies, reed marshes and flooded grassland, where the ground is soft and worms accessible. Here they nest in tussocks of grass or rush, usually laying four olive, blotched-brown eggs in their grass-lined nest.

> *Sittest at rest*
> *At safety neath the clump*
> *Of huge flag forrest that*
> *   thy haunts invest*
> *Or some old sallow stump*

wrote John Clare, in 'To The Snipe'. The females tend to be promiscuous at the beginning of the mating season, but eventually settle with one partner. On warm summer evenings the males dive in aerial courtship display, the outer tail feathers are spread and vibrate, making a drumming noise, which is partly territorial too, as they dive towards the ground.

> *Hearing the snipes' tail-feathers' drumming,*
> *Tiptoeing for a planet's coming.*

wrote Dorothy Ratcliffe in 'Home-Sickness', recalling precious memories of the Yorkshire countryside. In Victorian times it was generally believed that this unusual drumming sound was a vocal one. The shy snipe, with its seemingly overlong bill, is a conspicuous feeder, probing systematically into the mud with a sewing-machine action, for food, searching out insects and worms with its sensitive tip. They feed either in small groups or singly.

> *. . . by some ditch's side or little shallow lake*
> *Lie dabbling night and day the palate pleasing snite*

wrote Michael Drayton (1563-1631) in his 'Polyolbion'.
The plumage of the snipe is beautifully marked with lines and patches of buff, brown, black and pale chestnut with a strongly striped head. They often display on posts, uttering a distinctive call which changes to an agitated cry if their young are in danger.

In Scotland the drumming of snipe and the call of the partridge indicate dry weather and frost at night.

> *Snipes are calling from the trenches,*
> *Frozen half and half at flow,*

wrote Lord De Tabley in 'A Winter Sketch'.
The snipe was originally trapped by means of a springe, a noose fastened to an elastic body, which is drawn close with a sudden spring, whereby birds or small mammals can be easily caught as they walk along their familiar tracks.

> *Wilt thou set springes in a frosty night*
> *To catch the long-billed woodcock and the snipe.*

Medieval cooks would pluck, truss and roast the bird undrawn,

although the head was left on and the beak turned sideways to act as an efficient skewer. The snipe would be spit-roasted with fat bacon and ham and served on toast with a wine sauce. During the last century Salmi of snipe was a popular dish. The entrails, however, were removed before the snipe was half-roasted and cut into quarters and placed in a pot with two shallots, a glass of port wine, the juice of half a lemon, a little gravy, cayenne pepper, salt, and entrails finely chopped. It was stewed for ten minutes and served on a slice of brown bread, cut into quarters. Mrs Beeton suggested that 'one of these small but delicious birds may be given whole, to a gentleman; but in helping a lady... put only half on the plate.' She added, 'they should be sent to the table very hot and expeditiously, or they will not be worth eating'.

An eighteenth century sportsman's dish, considered to be expensive, except for a country gentleman, consisted of four snipe, two woodcocks, one pheasant, half a bottle of truffles, one bouquet of mixed herbs, half a bottle of sherry, a pinch of cayenne pepper and a teaspoon each of salt and pepper. This was served on toast with entrails of the Woodcocks and snipe with chopped truffles spread on it. Brillat Savarin's Mode was an unusual pheasant stuffing, consisting of two snipe, one thin slice of beef, a little suet, a few truffles, one slice of bread, one anchovy, one ounce of fresh butter and Florida oranges. It was prepared as follows: 'Take two snipes and draw them, put the bodies on one plate and the livers, etc, on another. Take the flesh of the birds, and mince it finely with a little beef suet, a few truffles, pepper and salt. Stuff the pheasant with this minced meat. Cut a slice of bread, larger considerably than the bird, and cover it with the livers, etc, and a few truffles, an anchovy and a little fresh butter will be an improvement. Put the bread, etc, into the dripping-pan. When the bird is roasted, place it on this preparation, and surround it with Florida oranges.'

The collective noun for a number of snipes on the ground is a walk, and a wisp for those in the air. A pair of dead birds is referred to as a couple as opposed to a brace, which is generally applied to other game-birds.

117

SPARROW

There is no bird half as harmless,
None so sweetly rude as you,
None so common and so charmless,
None of virtues nude as you.
But for all your faults I love you
For you linger with us still,
Though the wintry winds reprove you
And the snow is on the hill.
'To a Sparrow', FRANCIS LEDWIDGE

SPARROW *(Passer domesticus)*. Sparrow is a traditional name for various passerine and similar-looking birds figuring in three British species, hedge, house and tree sparrow;. The name goes back via Middle English 'sparewe' to Old English 'sparwa'. Sparrer is occasionally used. The house sparrow has been with us for centuries, favouring the habitat of man. The numerous common names attributed to the bird include thatch sparrow, grey spadger, spurgie, spurdie, lum lintie, cuddy and easing sparrow.

Widely distributed over the countryside, in farm buildings to city centres, there is no escaping this cheeky, chattering opportunist with its familiar plumage of warm brown nape and black bib of the male, contrasting with pale buff under-parts. The female is rather drab, which in no way hinders her ability to mate; noisy displaying flocks of males will chase a single bird for a considerable distance. They nest in buildings and hedgerows returning year after year, often producing three broods. The nest is mainly built by the male, a carelessly woven construction of hay and straw, lined with feathers. The eggs are greyish-blue in colour and finely speckled.

On me the chance-discovered sight
Gleamed like a vision of delight,

wrote William Wordsworth on discovering 'The Sparrow's Nest'. Sparrows have an unfortunate habit of taking over the nests of other birds, particularly swallows and martins. Various folk tales exist, in which they have been supposedly walled in with mud by the ejected occupant.

John Clare tamed a sparrow which he kept for three years: 'it would come when called and flew where it pleased'. Naturally he thought it 'a very cruel practice for the overseers of the parish to give rewards to boys to kill sparrows as they often do it very cruelly and cheat the overseers' ignorance many times in taking other harmless birds to pass them for sparrows to get the bounty.' He defended the sparrow, warning:

Hardy clowns! grudge not the wheat
Which hunger forces birds to eat:
Your blinded eyes, worst foes to,
Can't see the good sparrows do
Did not poor birds with watching rounds
Pick up insects from your grounds,
Did they not tend your rising grain,
You then might sow to reap again.

Farmers in the fifteenth century did not share his opinion, sending boys out in the fields with bows and arrows and much shouting, as William Cowper was later to record, adding his own harsh view of this chirpy bird:

The sparrow, meanest of the
*   feathered race,*
His fit companion finds in
*   every place,*
With whom he filches the
*   grain that suits him best,*
Flits here and there, and late returns to rest.

Sparrow charms were used to keep the birds away from the fields. The first one was used whilst the seeds were being sown. Three grains of corn were placed under the tongue and, at the end of the furrow, spat out and the following benediction uttered: 'No sparrow will come into the field, although the neighbouring one be full of sparrows.' An alternative charm was to place, upright in a field, a splinter from a piece of timber from which a coffin had been made.

In Somerset catching sparrows, known as bird batting or baiting, was carried out at night and required four people, a lantern, net, bell and pole. The unfortunate birds would most probably have been eaten in a pie or pickled.

> *The pie's in Home*
> *The birds begin to sing*
> *Isn't this a daddy-dish*
> *To set before a king?*

Sparrow pie was a popular winter dish. One recipe required a dozen birds, rump steak, a small bunch of savoury herbs, the peel of half a lemon, a slice of stale bread, half a cupful of milk, six eggs, pepper and salt, two ounces of butter and some puff pastry. A forcemeat made from the bread soaked in milk, the finely chopped herbs, minced peel of lemon, a piece of butter, pepper and salt and the whites of six boiled eggs, was mixed together and cooked in a stew pan for a few minutes, until it became stiff. Each small bird was stuffed with the mixture and placed in a dish lined with lightly fried rump steak, with a layer of sliced yolks of the hard-boiled eggs added and the whole covered with gravy – baking time one and a half hours.

A Georgian recipe of pickled sparrows advised one to draw the birds, cut off their legs, then make a pickle of water, a quarter of a pint of white wine, a bunch of sweet herbs, salt, pepper, cloves and mace. 'When it boils put in your sparrows, and when they are hot enough take them up, and when they are cold put them in a pot you keep them in, then make a strong pickle of rhenish wine and white wine; put in onion, a sprig of thyme and savoury, some lemon peel, some cloves, mace; boil all these together very well; then set it by till it is cold, and put it to your sparrows; once in a month new boil the pickle, and when the bones are dissolv'd they are fit to eat; put them in china saucers and mix with your pickles.'

William Wordsworth, translating a paragraph from the the work of the Venerable Bede, finds an unusual comparison:

Man's life is like a Sparrow, Mighty King,
That, stealing in, while by the fire you sit
Housed with rejoicing friends is seen to flit
Safe from the storm in comfort tarrying.
Here did it enter – there on hasty wing
Flies out, and passes on from cold to cold;
But whence it came, we know not, nor behold
Whither it goes.

In folklore the sparrow is a symbol of human attachment, lasciviousness, lowliness, melancholy and pugnacity. With the dove, swan, scallop shell, myrtle and goat, the sparrow is sacred to the goddess Venus. This association is mentioned in the long poem, 'The Parliament of Fowls' by Geoffrey Chaucer. 'The sparrow, Venus' son' and probably refers to the enthusiasm of the bird to breed. In passing one, should mention that sparrow eggs were said to be a popular aphrodisiac.

Seeing a sparrow on St Valentine's Day meant that a girl would marry a farmer or that she would marry a poor man but be happy. The poet Stephen Duck observed how the twittering birds take cover when rain is imminent:

. . . on a sudden, if a storm appears,
Their chirping noise no longer dins your ears:
They fly for shelter to the thickest bush;
There silent sit, and all at once is hush.

A further old country saying on a pending gale:

When sparrows ceasless chirp at dawn of day
And in their holes the wren and robin stay.

The anonymous poem 'Who Killed Cock Robin?' must be the worst possible introduction of this friendly little bird to children: 'I said the sparrow with my bow and arrow' – the very weapon used to destroy the sparrow in earlier days.

SPARROWHAWK

A sparhawk proud did hold in wicked jail
Music's sweet chorister, the Nightingale;
To whom with sighs she said: 'O set me free,
And in my song I'll praise no bird but thee.'
The Hawk replied: 'I will not lose my diet
To let a thousand such enjoy their quiet.'
'A Sparrow-Hawk,' ALFRED, LORD TENNYSON

SPARROWHAWK *(Accipiter nisus)*. The name sparrowhawk goes back via Middle English 'sperhauk' to Old English 'spearhafoc.' The species is said to be appropriately named because it preys largely on sparrows and other small birds. Such an obvious name, however, does not preclude a variety of regional ones such as gold tip, stone falcon, blue hawk, pigeon hawk, maalin, blue merlin and stannin hawk.

The male Sparrowhawk is called a musket in falconry, a name referred to in an anonymous fifteenth century poem:

I asked this birde what he meant;
He said, 'I am a musket gent;
For dread of death I am nigh shent, (destoyed)
Timor mortis conturbat me.'

Similarly in 'The Falcon' by Richard Lovelace:

Close-hooded all thy kindred come
To pay their vows upon thy tomb;
The hobby and the musket too
Do march to take their last adieu.

The bird is also known as hedge hawk, a reference to its hunting habits whereby it quarters the hedgerow, flushing out the small birds which are its main source of food. A surprise attack from a concealed perch on soaring, singing and display-ing birds over farmland and mixed woodland areas also guaran-tees a full stomach. In fact a good way to spot a sparrowhawk is to watch for a party of crows reeling round, birds being mobbed or thrushes 'chacking' in their distinctive way in the hedgerows.

The charming opening poem by Alfred, Lord Tennyson, illustrates the indifference of the sparrowhawk to the appeals of a nightingale – survival is more important than song.

The female sparrowhawk is larger than her partner, as in all raptors, and quite capable of taking on superior sized food such as the woodpigeon, which the male would shy away from. After a kill they take their prey to a stump or log to be plucked. This comparatively small but fast-flying bird of prey has been persecuted by farmers and gamekeepers for many years in the belief that it attacks game birds. This may be so, although studies now indicate that these make up a very small proportion of the sparrowhawk's diet. Pole traps, which are nothing more or less than gin or steel traps attached to wooden poles, were used by gamekeepers to catch the birds – they caused immense suffering because they did not kill immediately. Fortunately by 1904, thanks to Parliamentary legislation they were banned in Britain. Such traps have since been described as 'relics of barborous times'. Nevertheless it is said that illegal destruction still continues on some estates.

The sparrowhawk is a secretive bird who spends a great deal of time perched in its natural habitat – woodland – for which it is perfectly adapted with short, rounded wings and long tail, for flying between branches and tree trunks. Its long yellow legs and central toe – for catching and holding prey – indicate a bird eater. Apart from their size, the male and female are different in their colouring too. The male has bluish-grey plumage above and the bars on the white underside of its body are a deep orange, with brown wings and a tail which has dark bands. The female is duller and browner than the male, with grey-brown barring below and grey-brown above. The nest, which usually ends up as a large flat platform where the young in due course exercise their wings, is built several months before the eggs are laid.   The birds can be seen soaring in wide circles above the nesting area, flying with deliberate wing beats. There may be several nests, but during incubation the occupied nest of sticks, bark and dead leaves shows a distinctive white rim of feathers.

The superstitious must have regarded the sparrowhawk with some foreboding. According to John Aubrey's *Miscellanies* (1695): 'Not long before the Death of King Charles II a sparrow-hawk escaped from the Perch, and pitched on one of the Iron Crowns of the White Tower, and entangling its string in the Crown, hung by the heels and died. T'was considered very ominous, and so it proved.'

SWALLOW

She comes in the spring, all summer she stays,
And, dreading the cold, still follows the sun –
So, true to our Love, we should covet her rays,
And the place where he shines out, immediately shun.
'The Swallow', ABRAHAM COWLEY

SWALLOW *(Hirundu rustica)*. Swallow is the traditional name from Middle English 'swalowe,' from Old English 'sweal-we', the root of which literally meant cleft stick. It is also known as barn swallow, chimney swallow, house swallow, swallie and red-fronted swallow. Britain's swallows winter in South Africa, making this tremendous journey to compete for food, returning from March to May to mate. However 15 April was traditionally called Swallow Day, when they were said to appear. As everyone knows, 'One Swallow does not a summer make,' but to see three swallows, is a sign of good luck!

The mystery of the migration of birds caused much speculation amongst our ancestors many of whom, thinking that hibernation was a possibility, assumed that swallows either disappeared under the water or hid in holes in the ground until the spring. Olaus Magnus in *History of Nations* (1550) wrote: 'In Northern waters, fishermen often times by chance draw up in their nets an abundance of Swallows, hanging together like a conglomerated mass. In the beginning of Autumn, they assemble together amongst the reeds by ponds, where, allowing themselves to sink into the water they join bill to bill, and wing to wing and foot to foot' – one wonders what they actually saw! Gilbert White in his *Naturalist's Journal* (1776) speculated, 'if hirundines hide in rocks and caverns, how do they, while torpid, avoid being eaten by weasels and other vermin?'

Bad weather is the biggest killer of migrating swallows but, once home, they favour the haunts of man, returning to their old nesting grounds in farm buildings, through open doors or windows of sheds and outbuildings to fashion their familiar half-basin nests of mud and dry grass.

> *The swallow sweeps*
> *The slimy pool, to build his hanging house.*

wrote James Thomson. It is a sign of good luck if a swallow or a martin builds under the eaves of your house. Folklore endowed the birds with psychic powers; it was believed that they knew where foul deeds had been committed and they would nest on no house where cruelty was practised. Even more important to some 'In whatsoever house the swallow breedeth, the good man of the house is not made cuckold, what day soever he be married.' However, if anybody kills a swallow or destroys their nest, within the course of the year, they will break one of their bones or meet with some dreadful misfortune.

An old nest was recommended by John Hollybush in *The Homish Apothecary* for those needing help 'that hath squincy in the throat. Take the old nest of a swallow with all the substance (as clay, gravel sticks and feathers); do nothing but beat it and sift it through a coarse sieve, and put thereto grease and honey and make a plaster thereof. Then stroke it upon a cloth and lay it about his neck.' This was a mild remedy compared with a rather disgusting hangover cure 'for one that is or will be drunken. Take swallows and burn them, and make a powder of them; and give the man to drink thereof, and he shall never be drunk hereafter.' A broth made of crushed swallow was thought to cure epilepsy and stammering by sympathetic magic.

In folklore the swallow is a symbol of diligence, early morning, equality, fair-weather friends, good living, good luck, passage, hopefulness, protectors of young, providers, rebirth, spring, sunshine and wandering. If you dream of a swallow it indicates family happiness; if it is dead, lost affection; killing one, ingratitude; entering a house, good news from afar. In heraldry, it signifies one who is prompt and ready in the dispatch of his affairs.

Numerous proverbs and lore are associated with the swallow in spring and summer, including the Greek legend that the swallow was a form of Procne, daughter of the Athenian king Pandion (see Nightingale chapter). Delightful forecasts of the past are far removed from the sober pronouncements of today, such as this unusual verse indicating bad weather by E Darwin.

How restless are the snorting swine!
The busy flies disturb the kine;
Low o'er the grass the swallows ' wings
The cricket,too, how sharp he sings!

also:

When dip the swallows as the pool they skim.
And waterfowls their ruffled plumage trim

and

If swallows touch the water as they fly rain approaches.

An indication of fine weather from John Gay suggests:

When swallows fleet, soar high, and sport in air
He told us that the welkin would be clear.

Perhaps the most familiar quotation is from
The Winter's Tale by William Shakespeare,
connecting the bird with a spring flower.

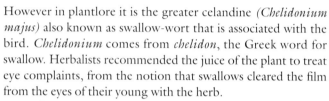

> *Daffodils.*
> *That come before the swallow dares, and take*
> *The winds of March with beauty.*

However in plantlore it is the greater celandine *(Chelidonium
majus)* also known as swallow-wort that is associated with the
bird. *Chelidonium* comes from *chelidon*, the Greek word for
swallow. Herbalists recommended the juice of the plant to treat
eye complaints, from the notion that swallows cleared the film
from the eyes of their young with the herb.

Underneath the streamlined blue-black wing feathers and
back is an elongated rich creamy-white vest which sweeps
down to the forked tail, topped by a blue collar, contrasting
vividly with the deep red plumage of a smart cravat and fore-
head. Described by Andrew Young in 'The Swallows' as:

> *Blue-winged snowballs! until they turned*
> *And then with ruddy breasts they burned;*
> *All in one instant everywhere,*
> *Jugglers with their own bodies in the air*

Ancient people believed that swallows carried two precious
stones inside their bodies – a red one to cure insanity and a
black one to bring good luck. These healing properties were
alluded to by Henry Wadsworth Longfellow in 'Evangeline':

> *Oft in the barns they climbed to the populous in the rafters*
> *Seeking with eager eyes that wondrous stone which swallows*
> *Bring from the shore of the sea to restore the sight of its*
> *   fledglings.*

Lucky was he who found a stone in the nest of the swallow!

SWAN

How lovely are these swans,
That float like high proud galleons
Cool in the summer heat,
And waving leaf-like feet
Divide with narrow breasts of snow
In a smooth surge
This water that is mostly sky;
So lovely that I know
Death cannot kill such birds,
It could but wound them, mortally.
'The Swans', ANDREW YOUNG

SWAN *(Cygnus olor)*. The name swan is unchanged since Old English times. In Britain there are three species: mute, Bewick and whooper. The male is known as a cob, the female a pen, and the young, cygnets. The mute swan *(Cygnus olor)* is also known as tame swan and wild swan. Mute is hardly descriptive of this impressive bird whose hoarse hiss, strangled trumpeting and growl when unduly disturbed not only alarms humans but birds and animals too. The speed with which they discourage intruders, particularly if they are nesting, flying and swimming quickly through the water with arched wings, breast thrust forward, head curved back and neck and feathers ruffled (called busking), is very intimidating.

He swells his lifted chest, and backward fling
His bridling neck between his tow'ring wings.

Shallow rivers, lakes and sheltered coasts are their habitat, where they drift along in majestic elegance, feeding on aquatic vegetation or upending in the water for hidden plant life. They graze on meadows or salt marshes too, consuming the occasional worm and snail. One delightful habit when they are drifting along in the water is to stretch out a foot to dry and then tuck it in among their feathers.

> *The stately-sailing swan*
> *Gives out his snowy plumage to the gale,*
> *And, arching proud his neck, with oary feet*
> *Bears forward fierce, and guards his osier-isle,*
> *Protective of his young*

wrote James Thomson in 'The Seasons'. Swans mate for life, building their nests by water margins, forming a depression in a splendid heap of vegetation in which five to eight chalky, greenish eggs are duly hatched.

The position of the nest was of interest to country people, as it was said the swan builds its nest high before floods, but low when there will not be unusual rains. Rain was thought to be imminent when:

> *The swans that sail along along the silvery flood,*
> *And dive with stretching necks to search their food,*
> *Then lave their backs with sprinkling dews in vain,*
> *And stem the stream to meet the promised rain.*

If a swan flies against the wind, it is a certain indication of a hurricane within twenty four hours, generally within twelve. In fact, if the bird flies at all it is a sign of rough weather. In Scotland, when they visit the Orkneys it is a sign of a continued severe winter.

In folklore the swan symbolizes beauty, cloud, death, dignity, eternity, excellence, grace, haughtiness, mist, music, poetry, prophecy, snow, wisdom, summer and solitude. In mythology the Swan is sacred to Aphrodite, Apollo, Jupiter, Leda, Orpheus, Venus and Zeus. It is a Christian symbol of Saint Cuthbert and Saint Hugh of Lincoln. Buddha was said to have been inspired to begin his teachings after rescuing a wounded swan. For thousands of years people have believed the swan sang, once, before dying:

The wild swan's death-hymn took the soul
Of that waste place with joy
Hidden in sorrow.

wrote Alfred, Lord Tennyson, in 'The Dying Swan'. Swans have appeared in legends from earliest times. In Greek mythology Zeus, supreme deity of ancient Greece, assumed the form of a swan, deceived and seduced Leda, daughter of King Thestius. She produced two eggs, from one emerged Castor and Clytemnestra, from the other, Pollux and Helen. In Northern folklore swan-maidens were fairies who could become maidens or swans at will by means of a swan-shift, a magic garment of swans' feathers. Many stories tell how the shift is stolen and the fairy held prisoner until rescued by a

knight. Variations on these tales involve an aversion to iron, often associated with magic, whereby the maiden, now married, is accidentally touched by the metal, flies away to a lake and vanishes.

Successive legends have been absorbed by different cultures, each substituting their own twists of fate. In Roman mythology, Cygnus was placed in the sky as a northern constellation in the Milky Way, which is also known as the Northern Cross or the Swan – by Christians it is called the Cross of Calvary.

Since ancient times the swan has enjoyed royal patronage. Edward I had a swan as his badge and, on the day he knighted his son, two swans with gilded beaks were brought to Westminster and upon these Edward took an oath against the Scots. Edward III passed protective legislation for the bird. During the reign of Edward IV it was decreed that, beside the king, only substantial freeholders might be granted a swan mark, designating ownership. Severe penalties were introduced by Henry VII for stealing the swan's eggs. The Crown still retains the right to the swans on the Thames between London Bridge and Henley-on-Thames, a right which it shares with the Vinters and Dyers Company. Today the young birds are still marked on their bill at the annual 'swan-upping'.

The swan seems to be one of a long list of birds hunted by fowlers since the Bronze Age, continuing through to Roman times, when it was the custom for large wildfowl to be hung for several days to tenderize them. If they were particularly 'high' a special strongly flavoured sauce consisting of pepper, lovage, thyme, dried mint, filbert nut, Jericho date, honey, vinegar, wine, liquamen, oil and mustard was served to mask any unpleasant flavour. Swan or peacock was served at banquets or special celebrations, dressed up as a processional centre piece for the top table.

Chief cooks were high-ranking household officials in England in the fourteenth century. Elaborate instructions were given for the dressing and carving of meats and birds. Although swan was expensive, tough and indigestible, it was served in full plumage at most great banquets because it was so

handsome. A cured skin with feathers and feathered head and beak with a bunch of tail feathers was kept for dressing the bird, which was presented garlanded and crowned on a silver or gold stand, with its wired wings outstretched, neck arched backwards, head erect, a piece of of blazing camphor or a wick in its beak.

Swan was usually served at royal banquets; it was also served on other occasions as an ordinary dish without the head. The swan stuffed with a seasoned forcemeat or little birds was roasted and served with a special sauce, chaudron, consisting of the bird's own guts, cut small and boiled in broth with its blood and vinegar and strong spices. During the last century a Norfolk recipe recommended cygnet eaten in December 'a capital and very magnificent Christmas dish' decorated with tiny swans cut out of white turnip. The recipe consisted of two pounds of chopped rump steak, one onion, spice, beaten cloves, one pound of butter and a little beef dripping for the forcemeat and basting. A strong beef gravy and half a pint of port wine were poured over the bird, which was served with hot currant jelly. Regardless of its protected status the swan often met a silent death by the hand of a poacher, yet others were restrained by their beauty:

> *. . . when alone at evening he watched*
> *Wild swans upon the reaches of a river,*
> *Grey cygnets in the twilight, and slid back*
> *The arrow to the quiver?*

Swans' eggs are said to have a strong flavour similar to goose. The shells were and are still used as decorative art forms.

STARLING

In an isolated tree a congregation
Of starlings chatter and chide,
Thickset as summer leaves, in garrulous quarrel:
Suddenly they hush as one, -
The tree top springs, -
And off, with a whirr of wings,
They fly by the score
To the holly-thicket.
'November,' ROBERT BRIDGES

STARLING *(Sturnus vulgaris)*. The name starling goes back
to the eleventh century 'staerling', young starling, formed with
the suffix ling from the primary name 'staer', which eventually
became stare, competing through the centuries with starling.
By 1850 it was rarely used, and starling became the established
form. Geoffrey Chaucer, in his *Parliament of Fowls*, used the
earlier name:

The stare, that the counsel can bewry (betray).

And much later, from 'The Rape of Lucrece' by Thomas
Heywood:

And from each bill let music shrill
Give my fair love good morrow.
Blackbird and thrush in every bush,
Stare, linnet, and cock sparrow.

Despite being included by the poet in such a chorus of song
birds, the starling is not exactly a noted songster; quite the
reverse in fact, managing to combine a series of trills, whistles
and rattles in somewhat unmelodious renderings. Nevertheless
the bird was greatly admired by the naturalist W H Hudson

(1841-1922). In an extract from Birds of London he wrote: 'you cannot listen to one of their choirs without hearing some new sound ... the clink clink as of a cracked bell, the low chatter of mixed harsh musical sounds, the kissing and finger cracking, and those long metallic notes, as of a saw being filed not unmusically, or (as a friend suggests) as of milking a cow into a tin pail.'

Allan Ramsay (1686-1758) was more than generous with his praise:

Of all the birds whose tuneful throats
Do welcome in the verdant spring,
I prefer the steerling's notes,
And think she does mostly sweetly sing.

Other names for the starling include starnel, black starling, sheep stare, sheeprack, starn, shepstarling and gyp. Many reflect an association with sheep, for starlings, being formidable feeders, alight on the back of the animal, picking off the ticks which plague it during the summer months. They also accompany grazing cows, looking out for insects in the grass as the herbage is torn from its roots.

The starling is widely distributed throughout the countryside and a familiar visitor in gardens, parks and towns.

135

They nest in buildings and woodlands, particularly vacated woodpecker holes, laying four to six blue eggs.

The starnel builds in chimneys from the view
And lays a egg like thrushes paley blue
Then breeds and flyes and in closes dwells
*   Where new made haystacks yield a pleasant smell*

wrote John Clare. In spring the male looks very attractive with a black, purple and green glossy bronze sheen replacing the dull winter plumage. Starlings have been roosting in London since the last century. Many of the communal winter roosts are located in plantations, city centres and reed beds when thousands of birds flock together. Smaller gatherings often take place on the way to larger roosts. The noise is tremendous but as the flocks assemble this rises in a crescendo, followed by an eerie, total silence, then off they go again to a final location. The birds are collectively known as a murmuration of starlings.

The starling is a great mimic, with an astonishing repertoire; the barking of a dog, bleating of sheep, mechanical sounds, notes and snatches of song, voices and of course the sound of other birds are all within its range:

They mimic in their glee,
With impudent jocosity

wrote Mary Webb. Such accomplishments ensured a caged existence for many birds. Being hardy, the starling could live in this captive state for a number of years. The bottom of the cage had a thick covering of coarse sand to prevent their claws from getting too long, and clods of earth, hopefully containing worms, which provided the bird with 'much benefit and enjoyment from its attempt to root them out'. W T Green, in *Birds I Have Kept,* quotes one such owner of a starling revealing a barbaric practice: 'nothing escapes his eye. He learns to pronounce words without having his tongue cut, which proves the uselessness of this cruel operation.'

Samuel Pepys, the diarist, when Secretary to the Admiralty, not only had a mynah bird, but also later acquired a starling through the good offices of a Mrs Martin – her husband was purser to the great man. The bird was a present in payment 'for little acts of kindness and six bottles of claret'. More surprising was the fact that it had belonged to the King who had kept it in his bedchamber!

When starlings assemble in flocks it is a sign of cold weather and when starlings and crows congregate together in large numbers, expect rain.

Fortunately for the starling, although prized by the Romans and cooked in a similar style to the thrush, it escaped the vagaries of more recent cooks, because the taste of the flesh was considered too bitter. However country people obviously had other ideas. On the Countryside March in London (1998) an elderly man spoke to me of eating roast starling earlier this century with his grandparents, a meal which he thoroughly enjoyed – until he discovered what he had eaten!

SONG THRUSH

Within a thick and spreading hawthorn bush,
That overhung a molehill large and round,
I heard from morn to morn a merry thrush
Sing hymns to sunrise, and I drank the sound
With joy; and often, an intruding guest,
I watched her secret toil from day to day.
'The Thrush's Nest', JOHN CLARE

SONG THRUSH *(Turdus philomelos)* Thrush is a traditional name going back through Middle English 'thrushe' to Old English 'prysce'. According to W B Lockwood, from the beginning of our language the present name, thrush, has competed with throstle, specifically song thrush. In districts where both names have been common, thrush has generally been restricted to missel thrush. In other parts where throstle was not in use the two species could be distinguished as song thrush and missel thrush, from which several hybrid forms have arisen, such as thrushel and thrustle. Missel thrush are known as thrush cock, storm cock, thrice cock and missel cock. Other common names for the song thrush include mavis, whistling thrush, garden thrush, throggie and trush drush. The song thrush is principally a resident bird, formerly located in woodland but now common in towns and gardens. It is easily recognized, with its upright stance, cloaked in warm-brown feathers on the upper parts of its body gradually blending with the distinctive pale buff, and dark speckled plumage of the under-parts. The creamy buff underwing is easily seen in flight. The song thrush is mainly a ground feeding bird, often seen moving across a lawn in short runs and hops, stopping occasionally to snatch a careless worm with unerring accuracy. The Poet Laureate, Ted Hughes, in his poem 'Thrushes', found them rather menacing:

> *Terrifying are the attent sleek thrushes on the lawn,*
> *More coiled steel than living – a poised*
> *Dark deadly eye, those delicate legs*
> *Triggered to stirrings beyond sense – with a start,*
> *a bounce, a stab*
> *Overtake the instant and drag out some writhing thing.*

The thrush is a regular visitor to the bird table, or more precisely the area around it, feeding on the morsels scattered by fellow diners. Generous owners of these highrise cafes may, later, be serenaded by a grateful bird – each song phrase of two or three syllables is repeated two to four times.

> *With glee, with glee, with glee,*
> *Cheer up, cheer up, cheer up, here*
> *Nothing to harm us, then sing merrily,*
> *Sing to the loved one whose nest is near.*

wrote W Macgillivray in 'The Thrush's Song'. The thrush is also partial to snails; the evidence is simply a pile of broken shells, relics of earlier snacks, where it has hammered the mollusc on a stone or garden step, enabling it to remove and digest the occupant – unless a keen-eyed blackbird swoops down first! The site is known as a thrush's anvil.

Nevertheless the thrush was a dainty morsel too. According to the book, *A Taste of History*, the Romans are said to have sacrificed their culinary skills to the presentation, ostentation and setting of their banquets. The dining room in which they took their meals, the triclinium, was so called because it was usual to arrange three couches around a central dining table, the fourth side remaining open for the serving slaves. One particular banquet, referred to as Trimalchio's Feast, had reached the third course when 'suddenly there was a loud roar and Laconian hounds burst into the room and began to run round the table followed by servants bearing an enormous platter on which lay a wild boar, two baskets lined with palm leaves hanging from its tusks – one filled with Syrian dates and the other with Theban dates. Little sucking pigs made out of pastry were offered to the guests who were allowed to take them away. Drawing a hunting knife a slave gave the wild boar a great stab in the belly and suddenly from the opening flew a number of thrushes. They tried in vain to fly out of the room but were caught in nets and offered to the guests.' Another Roman, Lucullus, was reputed to have had a private dining room set up inside an aviary so that he could enjoy a roast thrush, whilst the bird's relatives flew round above the table.

In earlier times the thrush was always a popular choice for the banquets of lay people and clergy, particularly as the latter were only allowed to eat 'two-legged' meat. A recipe published in 1814 in *Le Parfait Cuisinier*, includes the thrush, beginning modestly enough with a large olive, stuffed with anchovy, capers and oil placed in a boned and trussed garden warbler. The bird is then put inside a fat young wheatear which is placed inside a boned lark. The lark is then stuffed into a boned thrush which is put into a fat quail, wrapped in vine leaves, and placed inside a boned lapwing, which is put inside a boned golden plover. A partridge and woodcock follow, the latter rolled in breadcrumbs. Further birds include a boned teal, a guinea fowl, a tame duck, a fat boned fowl, a well-hung pheasant, a wild goose, a turkey and, finally, the rare bustard. The stuffed bird was then placed in a saucepan with onions stuffed with cloves, carrots, small squares of ham, celery and mignonette, closed off with pastry and cooked over gentle heat for ten hours!

Our ancestors had various methods for catching wild birds,

as Richard Barnfield describes in 'The Affectionate Shepherd':

> *Or if thou wilt go shoot at little birds*
> *With bow and bolt, the throstle-cock and sparrow*
> *Such as our country hedges can afford,*
> *I have a fine bow and an ivory arrow.*

Wild birds' eggs too were an important part of the diet – one egg seems a small offering but a nestful was a different matter. Unfortunately, Flambée Thrush is still a popular dish in parts of Europe.

Country people would also catch wild birds which they would keep in a cage near the house, so that they could enjoy their beautiful song.

> *Summer is coming, summer is coming,*
> *I know it, I know it, I know it,*
> *Light again, leaf again, life again, love again,*
> *Yes, my wild little poet.*

wrote Alfred, Lord Tennyson, in 'The Throstle'.

There were those who believed that the singing of the bird at a certain time in the day could forecast rain. It was said that when the thrush sings at sunset, a fair day will follow, and that the mistle thrush sings particularly loud and clear before rain.

The strangest superstition that prevailed in many parts of England was that the song thrush acquired new legs and cast the old ones at the age of ten years.

WHEATEAR

The name of wheat-ears on them is ycleped
Because they come when wheat is yearly reaped
Six weeks or thereabouts they are catched there
And are well-nigh eleven months, God knows where.
'Rara Avis', JOHN TAYLOR

WHEATEAR *(Oenanthe oenanthe)*. The name Wheatear seems to have appeared in 1591 as 'thrie whekeres' which is believed to be a misprint for 'wheteres'. it was followed in 1653 by Wheatears', then by 1661 we read 'Wheat-ear is a bird peculiar to Sussex . . . it is so called, because fattest when wheat is ripe . . . whereon it feeds' – they actually prefer insects and worms. By 1678 it had acquired a further two names, fallow-smich and white-tail. From these, the eighteenth century naturalist Pennant took wheatear which thereafter became the standard name.

Francis Willughby in his *Ornithology* (1678) explained that in Sussex the wheatear is so called because 'at the time of the harvest they wax very fat'. The name in fact derives from Middle English 'whiters', literally white arse – the word arse

was not at that time thought to be vulgar. The rump and the base of the tail flash conspicuously white as the bird flies a little above the ground – which explains white arse, white foot and white tail as common names. The habitat and scratchy song of the bird have inspired names such as chach, chock check bird, horse smatch, stanechacker and hedge chicker. It is also known as fallow finch, fallow smiters and furze chat and it was said to 'haunt old ruins graveyards and cairns and has gotten a bad name'.

The wheatear is among the earliest spring arrivals, often reaching the south coast of England by mid-March. They are typical birds of open country, widely distributed in the Northern hemisphere, making long migratory flights to Africa. In Britain they often deliver their song, a harsh 'chack', from a hovering flight over moorland, heath, hills, sandy coastlands and even mountain tops. A favourite perch of this very attractive bird is the top of a post or on a stone wall, where they sing and display their blue-grey back, black wings and eye mask and delicate orange breast plumage. Their long black legs give them an upright and rather superior air. The female is a more buffish-brown colour. As they take flight the white rump is quite conspicuous, in contrast to the black 'T' shape on the tail. They nest in sheltered places such as natural crevices in a hole, rock or wall, even a rabbit burrow. The nest is loosely made of dry grass, lined with feathers, hair or rabbit fur, in which five or six pale blue eggs are hatched. The parents are very wary and go to great lengths not to give any clue to the whereabouts of their nest.

In earlier times they were obviously quite a common bird as Thomas Fuller in his *Worthies* (1672) lists the 'natural commodities of Sussex as Iron, Wheatears, Carps and Talc'. As Walter de la Mare commented later in his book, *Come Hither*, It is hard to believe that a bird not much larger than a nightingale, was (and may still be) a glutton's delicacy. I myself have seen poulterers' shops (in 'Stupidity Street') festooned with skylarks as if holly at Christmas. Apart from their singing and their beauty, none but a gormandizer, surely, hungers after little birds (e.g. wagtails). 'Four wheatears on a glutton's dish is a horrid sight; four hungry men sitting round a table with a fat roast goose in the middle is less so.' John Taylor in his poem 'Rara Avis' seems as if he is writing with enthusiasm based on experience:

> There were rare birds I never saw before,
> The like of them I think no more
> They are called wheat-ears, less than lark or sparrow,
> Well-roasted in the mouth they taste like marrow,
> When one 'tis in the teeth it is involved
> Bones, flesh, and all, is lusciously dissolved.

In earlier times the cooking, and in particular the preparation of the wheatear, was quite rudimentary. 'Do not draw them pluck and wipe them, very clean outside; truss them, legs close to the body, and the feet pressing upon the thighs; skin the head and neck, and bring the beak round under the wing. Spit them on a small bird spit, flour them, and baste well with butter.' The birds were served on toast with the crusts removed with gravy and garnished with slices of lemon. Mrs Beeton's recipe on the other hand advised gutting and cleaning 'truss them like larks, put them to a quick fire, and baste them well with fresh butter. When done, which will be in about 20 minutes, dish them on fried bread-crumbs, and garnish with slices of lemon.'

Country boys enjoyed bird-nesting although there were some nests, for superstitious reasons, they avoided. Two birds in particular are referred to by Edward Armstrong in *Folklore of Birds*; 'Perhaps the stonechat and wheatear became associated with the devil because their calls, suggestive of pebbles being knocked together, heard by timorous people in desolate places, may have aroused apprehension of unseen evil presences moving close at hand . . . quasi-human bird utterances are commonly regarded as uncanny and devilish; because the devil is conceived as the personification of evil and a being with partly human and partly animal characteristics, birds which seem to partake of two natures are associated with it.'

WOODCOCK

WOODCOCK *(Scolopax rusticola)*. The name woodcock has been used since earlier times to denote the name of the species, going back via Middle English 'wudecoc' to Old English 'wuducocc', a term known since AD1050. The word cock used to refer, with other game birds, to woodcock; Reference is made in the record of a cockshoot in 1530 of a 'broad way or glade in a wood, through which woodcock etc, might dart or 'shoot'; so as to be caught by nets stretched out across the opening'. A popular time of year would seem to have been 'if anye Easterly wind be aloft', from about two or three weeks before Michaelmas up until Christmas. It was also known as wudusnite, literally wood snite – woodsnipe, great snipe, long-bill and quis.

The woodcock is rather a retiring bird, preferring the quiet seclusion of damp woodland and coppices where it can hide during the day, beautifully camouflaged with its dark brown mottled back, rust coloured shaded wings enfolding a breast of creamy-buff plumage. Sharp, glinting, large eyes, reputed to have 360° vision, are well set back on a striped and barred head supporting a handsome bill. The nest is often sited in a hollow near the base of a tree, or the shelter of overhanging under-growth, and consists mainly of dead leaves and a sparse lining of dry grass or withered leaves.

Woodcock lay two clutches of four eggs annually, which they arrange in a circle; the ground colour is creamy-white through a rich buff, to olive-brown with reddish-brown markings. If danger threatens the nesting woodcock, they have the most charming habit, which may involve several journeys, of flying, carrying their young between their legs, to safety. The collective noun for woodcock is a fall.

The resident population of woodcock is increased by flocks of winter migrants which were formerly believed to arrive overnight on an easterly wind in October, around All Hallows (31 October). In earlier times there was much speculation as to where or whether woodcock spent the summer on the moon. John Gay in 'The Shepherds Week' (1714) commented:

> *Some think to northern coasts their flight they tend*
> *Or, to the moon in midnight hours ascend*

This strange idea of moon migratation was debated by Olaus Magnus in the sixteenth century and continued to divide thinkers until the eighteenth century. Charles Morton, in the *Harleian Miscellany,* mused on the original idea by suggesting that the birds would take about two months each way for the journey; with a three-month break on their lunar outpost.

> *A bird of passage gone as soon as found*
> *Now in the moon perhaps, now underground.*

wrote the poet Alexander Pope, adding further literary input.

The arrival of the woodcock was of particular significance in country lore. If they appeared early, fine weather and a good harvest could be expected; however, if the hay had not been gathered in by the time the woodcock appeared, ruin was inevitable, especially if oats were sown late in the spring.

> *Cuckoo oats and Woodcock hay*
> *Make a farmer run away.*

Weather was the least of the woodcock's problems. Nets, traps and guns were used over the centuries to bring this comparatively small game bird to the table. By the turn of the twentieth century tilted platform traps were in use, which were very attractive to the birds in the cold grip of winter. A tall basket

was secured in the fork of a tree with a lid forming an oscillating board. On one side of the upper surface was fastened a mesh-covered box containing bilberries. As the hungry woodcock leaned over to get at the fruit, the lid tilted and the bird was pitched into the basket.

John Gay, in an extract from 'Rural Sports', recalls the flight of the bird when shot-guns dominated the countryside.

> *The woodcock flutters; how he wav'ring flies*
> *The wood resounds: he wheels, he drops, he dies.*

An exclusive club was formed and to qualify for membership one had to have shot two birds with a double-barrelled gun. On 20 November 1829 it was recorded that a William Chantrey 'killed in one shot two Woodcock' in the new plantations on the Holkham estate. According to the article 'the deed was forever commemorated by the hand of the sculptor himself in a low relief at Holkham Hall, Norfolk.' The flight of the woodcock varies, and is often quite rapid, but when undisturbed it can be rather slow and wavering. Nevertheless, the only time the male openly appears is at dusk when he performs a display, flying low over woodland territory in a regular circuit, flapping broad wings in a slow rhythm, known as roding, simultaneously emitting a 'deep repeated croaking growl'. They are slower than the partridge or pheasant when taking off from bracken, for instance, but very much faster among the trees. The Poet Laureate, John Betjeman (1906-1984), was mindful of the King's respect and care of game birds on his Sandringham estate, when in his poem, 'Death of George V', he wrote movingly of:

> *Spirits of well-shot woodcock, partridge and snipe*
> *Flutter and bear him up the Norfolk sky.*

Since Roman times the bird has been considered a source of food, invariably roasted. By the end of the 13th century the price of woodcock sold in London was fixed at 'a penny halfpenny apiece', against pheasant at fourpence and a heron sixpence.

Eighteenth century cooks followed the example of their predecessors in their preparations, merely plucking and wiping the bird clean and trussing it with the legs close to the body (first skinning the head and neck) and placing the beak round under the wing. However, they recommended that the bird be enclosed in a layer of bacon before being spit-roasted; while a slice of buttered toast placed underneath the bird caught the entrails. After basting the woodcock for twenty minutes, the toast was cut into quarters, placed in a dish and covered with butter and gravy, topped by the woodcock with their bills facing outwards. Served with plain butter sauce in a tureen. Salmi of Woodcocks required the whole bird to be quartered and cooked with two shallots, a glass of port wine, juice of half of lemon, a little gravy, salt and cayenne pepper. The *Larousse Gastronomique* gives thirty-three recipes for woodcock.

The name woodcock is also slang for a simpleton from the belief that woodcock are without brains. This belief was born from the fact that they were easily trapped by nets or snares when driven from their hiding place or making low flights during the mating season; a belief well established in the medieval period. The writers Beaumont and Fletcher would have been widely understood by their readers in the comedy T*he Loyal Subject* (1618) when they wrote:

> *Go like the Woodcock*
> *And Thrust your head into the noose.*

Also in William Shakespeare's, *The Taming of the Shrew* 'O this woodcock! what an ass it is'. *In Much Ado About Nothing* he mentions the bird 'Shall I not find a woodcock too?' also in Hamlet, when Polonius tells his daughter that protestations of love are 'springes to catch woodcocks'.

GREEN WOODPECKER

... from wintry sleep
Awake her insect prey; the alarmed tribes
Start from each chink that bores the mouldering stem:
Their scattered flight with lengthening tongue the foe
Pursues, joy glistens on her verdant plumes,
And brighter scarlet sparkles on her crest.
'Walks in a Forest', THOMAS GISBORNE

GREEN WOODPECKER *(Picus viridis)*. The green wood-pecker was well known to early naturalists and mentioned by the author J Palsgrave in 1530. It has numerous country names, many of which derive either from the bird's reputation as a weather prophet or the sound of its voice. Whilst it would be impossible to list them in their entirety they include awl-bird, woodwale, popinjay, yaffle, laughing bird, hecco and hew-hole. Victoria Sackville-West in 'The Garden' indicated her preference for the familiar laughing call for which it is renowned:

The orchard where the yaffle and the jays
Streak a bright feather as they take to wing.

Reginald Arkell in a verse from his amusing poem 'Green Woodpecker', also favoured the name:

His cap it were scarlet,
His jacket were green –
The finest old Yaffle
That ever were seen.
He laughed and he laughed
As he sat on the bough,
But I couldn't make sense
Of that Yaffle, nohow.

149

Andrew Marvell used an older name, hewel, in 'Upon Appleton House', and describes the bird's climbing technique. With the assistance of its zygodactyl toes, it is able to search for food and extract ants, its favourite food, and other insects with its strong beak and long tongue.

> *But most the hewel's wonders are,*
> *Who here as the holtfelster's care.*
> *He walks still upright from the root,*
> *Meas'ring the timber with his foot;*
> *And all the way to keep it clean*
> *Doth from the bark the wood-moths glean*

Andrew Young's poem, 'The Green Woodpecker' refers to the bird as a Popinjay, a name which was in popular use since the fourteenth century:

> *Whether that popinjay*
> *Screamed now at me or his mate*
> *I could not rightly say,*
> *Not knowing was it love or was it hate.*
> *I hoped it was not love*
> *But hate that roused that gaudy bird.*

The green woodpecker, which is usually found in dense woodland, parkland and commons, is a rather shy bird, more often heard drumming a distinctive methodical beat, than seen. Colourful in bright green plumage with primary feathers of brown with white spotting and what appears to be a crimson, reversed baseball cap, mottled with grey, stretching from beak to nape. The male sports a matching red central streak on a dark moustache below a black eye-band. In flight, the brilliant yellow rump is very conspicuous as it swoops and glides with the occasional short bursts of flapping. In spring the male and female chase in courtship, and display with beaks held up and heads swaying. The trunks and thick branches of oak and birch trees are their favourite nesting sites where they hammer out, with their beaks, a cavity and prepare a nest of wood chippings in which they lay four to seven glossy white eggs.

In mythology Picus, son of Saturn, and in some traditions the first king of Italy, was a famous soothsayer who derived omens from the movement of birds, making use in his prophetic art of a woodpecker (picus). He was represented in a primitive manner as a wooden pillar with a woodpecker perched on top – later as a young man with a woodpecker on his head. Picus loved Pomona, the tree goddess, but Circe the sorceress also loved him, and when he rejected her she changed him into a woodpecker who, however, retained the prophetic powers he had had as a man.

In the legends of the woodpecker there seems to be a combination of various popular beliefs. The woodpecker is alleged to be the bird which helped the wolf feed Romulus and Remus, twin sons of Silvia and Mars. A Roman coin is said to exist, depicting two woodpeckers in a sacred fig tree with a wolf, feeding the two boys beneath the branches. The bird is also associated with water – hence the names rainbird, weathercock and wet bird. The familiar laughing call is viewed as the sign of a shower or as another source phrased it: 'the cry of a woodpecker denotes much wet'. Unfortunate too if you see a woodpecker on St Valentine's Day, for you will never marry.

Our ancestors seemed to have enjoyed the taste of woodpecker. It was prepared and cooked in a similar way to the blackbird and the thrush, drawn, usually wrapped in bacon and spit-roasted with the occasional basting according to the size of the bird.

WREN

By the trim hedgerow bloomed with purple air;
Where, under the thorns, dead leaves in huddle lie
Packed by the gales of autumn, and in and out
The small wrens glide
With a happy note of cheer.
'November', ROBERT BRIDGES

WREN *(Troglodytes troglodytes)*. Troglodytes means cave dweller. Wren is a traditional name via Middle English 'wrenne', from Old English 'wrenna'. The bird has many alternative names which either refer to its short tail, diminutive size, voice or are simply affectionate, as in Bobby, Kitty, Sally or the familiar Jenny Wren. Others, from a wide variety of names include wran, wrannock, stumpy, chitty, titmeg, gilliver wren, puggie wren and cutty. The tiny, elusive, excitable wren, with its explosive calls and song, tends to sing higher up in the trees and bushes as spring progresses, warning other birds not to infringe on its territory. John Clare in his poem 'The Wren' posed a question:

Why is the cuckoos melody preferred
And nightingales' sick song so madly praised
In poets' rhymes is there no other bird
In nature's minstrelsy that hath not
     raised
One's heart to extasy and mirth as
     well . . .

It is usually seen darting between clumps of plants in search of live food. The most distinctive feature of the wren is its short, cocked tail. It has a red-brown back and wings with darker bars and buff-coloured breast plumage, apart from the goldcrest the wren is the smallest British bird.

They nest in woodlands and gardens, favouring holes and crevices in ivy-clad trees and walls, as well as remote sea cliffs. As part of his courting ritual, the male builds several nests of which the female will line one with feathers. The eggs are white with red speckles, five or six in number, even though the nursery rhyme, 'The Dove and the Wren', suggests otherwise. Here the dove complains:

> 'Coo, coo; what shall I do?
> I can scarce maintain two.'
> 'Pooh, poo! says the wren; I have got ten,
> And keep them all like gentlemen.'

Despite fluctuations in the wren population, even after a severe winter it is said to be the commonest British bird. For warmth and protection in harsh weather conditions the birds roost communally in natural or artificial sites, such as a nest box, where up to forty birds have been recorded in one evening. In folklore, apart from the Druids who regarded it as a bird of prophecy and the Irish, as a magician or a sorcerer, the wren was believed to be a sacred and protected bird who was sacrificed on St Stephen's Day (December 26). In Christian legend it was believed that the wren alerted the guards when Saint Stephen attempted to escape from imprisonment, and indirectly brought about the death of the first English martyr. It was the custom among communities to hunt the bird with birch rods and stone it to death in commemoration of the saint's martyrdom. The tiny decorated corpse was carried about by luck-bringing Wren Boys chanting:

> The Wren, the Wren, the King of All Birds
> St Stephen's Day was caught in the furze
> Although he be little, his honour is great
> Therefore good people, give us a treat.

There were variations on this ceremony, such as one practised in Wales whereby a boy carried a decorated cage, shaped like a house, containing a live wren, which he paraded round the village. On seeing the beribboned prison one was supposed to say, 'Pleased to see the king', as the boy sang:

> *Come and make your offering*
> *To the smallest yet the king.*

A donation was the price of the wren's freedom.

An alternative earlier ceremony blending pagan and Christian practise was to carry the dead bird on a pole to the churchyard. Wren-hunting ceremonies were practised in many European countries. In the south of France, for instance, they would bear the captured wren, suspended as if it was a heavy burden, on a long pole carried on the shoulders of two men through the streets, then it was weighed on a large pair of scales – a noisy celebration followed. The custom of wren-hunting was practised in ancient Greece and Rome, where the bird was known as little king. According to the ornithological authority Edward Arnold, the wren cult is thought to have reached the British Isles during the Bronze Age from the Mediterranean. The timing, around New Year, is significant in that it represents the death of dark earth powers and the beginning of a new season of light and life.

The superstitious believed it unlucky to destroy the nest of wren or robin as a house fire, the breaking of crockery or a death would follow, as the anonymous verse (1770) implies:

> *I found a robin's nest within our shed,*
> *And in the barn a wren has young ones bred,*
> *I never take away their nest, nor try*
> *To catch the old ones, lest a friend should die.*

If a child killed a wren it was punished with the fire of St Lawrence – a skin complaint. For an adult the punishment was more drastic – they would be struck by lightning.

> *Kill a robin or a wren,*

Never prosper, boy or man.

An old Scottish rhyme curses those who would harm the bird:

Malaisons, malaisons mair that ten
That harry Our Lady of Heaven's wren.

For a bride to hear a wren singing in a hedge on the way to her wedding is a particularly lucky omen.

There are many rhymes and folk tales associating the wren with the robin. For instance, a marriage, commencing:

Says Robin to Jenny, 'If you will be mine,
We'll have cherry tart, and drink currant wine.'
So Jenny consented – the day was proclaimed . . .

Unfortunately the happy marriage state was brief, one day . .

A hawk with Jenny flew away;
And Robin, by the cruel sparrow
Was shot quite dead with bow and arrow.

During marital bliss:

The robin and the wren
They fought upon the porridge pan;
But ere the robin got the spoon,
The wren had eat the porridge down.

Our Lady's hen and cutty quean were folk names for the bird. The latter appears in a different form in part of another marriage rhyme when the faithless wren gives her ring to a soldier. Robin asks:

And where's the ring that I gied ye,
That I gied ye, that I gied ye,
Ye little cutty quyne?

YELLOWHAMMER

Even in a bird, the simplest notes have charms
For me: I love the yellowhammer's song.
When earliest buds begin to bulge, his note,
Simple, reiterated oft, is heard
On leafless briar, or half-grown hedgerow tree;
Nor does he cease his note till autumn's leaves
Fall fluttering round his golden head so bright.
'Birds of Scotland', JAMES GRAHAME

YELLOWHAMMER *(Emberiza citrinella)*. Yellowhammer was first recorded in 1587, although in 1544 'yelow ham, yowlryng' was mentioned by W Turner. By 1657 it had become 'yellowham bird,' surviving in parts of the South of England as yellow an-bird and yell am-bird. Yellowhammer is a corruption of yellow ammer – the German word for bunting, hence the common name yellow bunting. By 1883 yellow hammer was the accepted form and the present name established itself in ornithological books earlier this century. Nevertheless there are numerous country names for the bird, many reflecting the brilliant yellow plumage such as yellow amber, yellow yorling, yellow ring, gold spink, goldie, scotch canary, bessie buntie and gladdie. From the dark, crooked markings on the eggs, came scribbling lark, writing lark, writing master and scribbler.

Five eggs, pen scribbled o'er with ink their shells
Resembling writing-scrolls, which Fancy reads
As Nature's poesy and pastoral spells –
They are the yellow hammer's

The variable rhythm of the yellowhammer's song provided delightful longer names – little-bit-of-bread-and-no-cheese, may-the-devil-take-you, pretty-pretty-creature and cheeser. Early English country names included yellow yorling and yellow pate, a name favoured by Michael Drayton in 'Polyolbion':

> *The yellow pate, which though she hurt the blooming tree*
> *Yet scarce hath any bird a finer pipe than she.*

However Samuel Coleridge Taylor was less flattering:

> *The spruce and limber yellowhammer*
> *In the dawn of spring and sultry summer,*
> *In hedge or tree the hours beguiling*
> *With notes as of one who brass is filing.*

In folklore the yellowhammer was believed to be sacred to the sun god; but like the wren, he paid for such an association by being persecuted. In the north of Scotland boys played a game called spangie-hewit during which they shouted and screamed what was said to be a 'rhyme of reproach' to the yellow yorling or yellowhammer, since the bird was said to be 'cursed by the causeless hate of every School boy'. The bird was alleged to have devil-toad associations and was supposed to say 'De'il, de'il, de'il tak ye'. The yellowhammer cursed in vain, because not only did the children destroy its nest, but any birds they were able to catch would either be strung up or have their head jerked off with a piece of string, as the bloodthirsty youngsters taunted it with the following rhyme:

> *Half a paddock, half a toad,*
> *Half a yellow yorling:*
> *Drinks a drap o'the de'il's*
> *   bluid*
> *Every May morning.*

An alternative rhyme also included the badger:

> *The brock and the toad and the yellow yorling*
> *Tak a drap of the devil's ilka May morning.*

The male yellowhammer is a rather slim, long-tailed bird with a bright lemon-yellow head and breast, with a chestnut-coloured streaked back – the female is much duller.

> *Yellow-hammers, gold-headed, russet-backed,*
> *They fled in jerky flight before my feet*

wrote Andrew Young in 'The Yellow-hammers'. In flight their unmarked rusty rump and white streaked tail are particularly attractive, as they fly over their territory, which is mainly farmland, scrub and hill country, from where they often make long, circular flights. During courtship rituals the male can be very aggressive, performing aerial acrobatics, twisting and turning to impress a prospective mate. Yellowhammers build low down in hedges or grassy clumps, constructing a bulky nest of straw or dried grasses.

> *There, at a bramble-root, sunk in the grass,*
> *The hidden prize, of withered field-straws formed,*
> *Well lined with many a coil of hair and moss,*
> *And in it laid five red-veined spheres*

wrote James Grahame of the pleasure in finding a yellowhammer's nest. Collecting birds eggs was once an innocent country past-time, when chidren would remove one egg thinking it would not be missed, but some collectors were too greedy and it was rightly banned.

> *The yellow hammer never makes a noise*
> *But flyes in silence from the noisy boys*
> *The boys will come and take them every day*
> *And still she lays as none were taken away*

As John Clare observed.

Better one bird in the hand than ten in the wood:
Better for birders, but for birds not so good.
'Of Bird and Birders' JOHN HEYWOOD (1497-1580)